BY KIMBERLY WILSON
tranquilitydujour.com

Copyright 2014 by Kimberly Wilson

All rights reserved. This book may not be reproduced in whole or in part, stored in a retrieval system, or transmitted in any form or by any means—electronic, mechanical, or other—without written permission from the publisher, except by a reviewer, who may quote brief passages in a review.

Tranquilista, Tranquilologie, Tranquil Space, Hip Tranquil Chick, TranquiliT, and Tranquil Space Foundation are registered trademarks.

DISCLAIMER: This publication contains the opinions and ideas of its author. The advice contained herein is for informational purposes only. Please consult a medical professional before beginning any diet or exercise program. The author disclaims all responsibility for any liability, loss, risk, injury, or damage resulting from the use, proper or improper, of any of the contents contained in this book. Every effort has been made to ensure that the information contained in this book is complete and accurate.

First printing, September 2014
ISBN: 978-0-692-32339-7
Printed in the United States of America

iPhoneography by Kimberly Wilson
Text design and typography by Christy Jenkins • holeyheart.com

Manifesto

I believe in handwritten notes. I believe in using china at every meal. I believe in the healing power of bubble baths. I believe that animals are to be loved, not used. I believe that you're never too old to wear a tutu. I believe that Paris holds the key to my heart. I believe in stargazing around a campfire. I believe in lazy Sunday mornings. I believe that magic happens on the yoga mat. I believe in high tea at all times of the day. I believe in living life full out. I believe in sharing deep thoughts with my journal. I believe in donning noir and living pink. I believe that glitter and washi tape make life better. I believe in lighting candles every day. I believe that paint, collage, and markers make for hours of fun. I believe in pink and white twinkle lights. I believe in seeking balance between doing and being. I believe in the power of one person to make a difference. I believe that a home filled with books is a happy one. I believe in cat eyes and red lips à la Parisian chic. I believe in brunch and belly laughs with girlfriends.

This book is dedicated to the readers of *Tranquility du Jour* who inspire me to do more, be more, and give more. Thank you for reading and sharing this journey with me.

Table of Contents

Chapter 1: Bonjour 8
Chapter 2: My Story 15
Capter 3: Yoga 47
Capter 4: Lifestyle 67
Chapter 5: Creativity 85
Chapter 6: Entrepreneurship 101
Chapter 7: Activism 121
Chapter 8: Mindfulness 141
Chapter 9: Travel 157
Chapter 10: Epilogue 179
Appendix 185
    Monthly, Weekly + Daily Tranquility Tools 185
    Current Day in the Life 190
    52 Tranquility Tips 192
    Pen Month's Dreams 195
    Gratitude List 196
    Tranquility Thoughts 198
    Kale Chips/Green Juice 200
    Photo Credits 204
    Index 204
Acknowledgements 210
About the Author 213

CHAPTER 1:
Bonjour

Tranquility is the quality of calm within a full and meaningful life. —*Moi*

In the Beginning

When I began a blog called *TranquiliT Thoughts* in the fall of 2004, I was eager to craft a writing practice through self-expression and reach like-hearted souls. Feeling the lonely effects of years as a ruminating introvert, I had hopes of finding my tribe in this online format.

Over the years I've received love notes from women around the globe expressing gratitude for the *Tranquility du Jour* blog and podcast. They always seem to come at the perfect time: when I'm feeling behind, stuck, or less than stellar. There's Ines in Portugal who wrote, "I just can't stop reading your blog. In fact, you've led me to take my dreams more seriously, to believe in them, to believe they can come true!" There's Marie in Miami: "I first discovered your podcast as I rummaged through iTunes searching for the perfect podcast. Then I discovered your blog. Ever since then my creative life has skyrocketed." And there's Brandi in Los Angeles: "My confidence level is higher because you have brought to me an enormous variety of female professionals to learn from on an intimate level. In my loneliest, moodiest, most confused, PMS-driven, and blah moments, I always run to your archive and find a Band-Aid."

Musings began with a focus on yoga lifestyle and ultimately provided fodder for my first book, *Hip Tranquil Chick*. I'd sit down in front of my laptop, pull up blogger.com, and watch the blinking cursor. I'd then wait for the muse to hit. And wait. Often she appeared. Sometimes not, so I shut the laptop and moved on, awaiting a future visit.

Posts trickled out once or twice a week for the first few years and I began receiving comments from readers as far as Australia and the United Kingdom. *How had they found me? Was I offering them something they needed? Would they like me if we met?* I wondered. As a lifelong journal writer, this online space felt exposing and rewarding at the same time. I was completely naked before an audience open to a worldwide readership.

With the launch of a podcast one year later, the connection to more tranquility-seekers grew. With the click of a button, one could read my thoughts and ideas on the blog or listen to musings and interviews of people creating businesses, making art, and writing books on the podcast. I slowly began to develop a voice—writing and beyond.

*TranquiliT Thought*s then transitioned into the *Hip Tranquil Chick* namesake fueling more yoga lifestyle tips. After the release of my second book, *Tranquilista*, the blog transitioned to *Tranquility du Jour* to accommodate the infusion of different topics such as style, DIY, activism, and creativity beyond the realm of yoga.

While completing graduate studies in social work, I created an e-course, *Tranquilologie*, with 96 essays {eight monthly} for living tranquilly. I turned it into a hardcover, limited-edition book and set off in a vintage camper on the two-month Tranquility Tour hosting 23 Pop-Ups across the country and Canada. The Pop-Ups were a three-hour summit of mindfulness, yoga, and art journaling and took place in living rooms, historic buildings, churches, and restaurants secured by gracious hosts. Meeting longtime readers in cities such

> The decade of posts reflects a continued evolution of interests, passions, struggles, and successes.

as Calgary, Los Angeles, and Philly during this adventure solidified the power of penning prose onto the Internet.

Blogging Inspiration

Despite the sophistication of blogging now, I've never been one to write, lay out, and schedule posts in advance. Nope, no blog editorial calendar for me. I prefer to see what the muse brings. If I have something to say, I want to share it right at that moment. Kind of like a child who can't wait to show Mom what was created in school that day. Or, honestly, every time I try to surprise, I'm way too excited not to say, "I may or may not have gotten you a gift card to your favorite restaurant!"

Sure, there are times that I sit down and have a story or essay in mind. Often it's a picture I've posted on Instagram that fuels my piece. Over the past few years I have transitioned to columns, offering specific topics on certain days—from Mindful Monday to Friday's Week in Review. This helps keep the musing fresh and focused on one subject that resonates with that specialized snapshot of daily life.

When I hear that the blog has helped infuse a reader's day with inspiration, I feel my ongoing dedication to wordsmithing is making a difference. And when a reader shares that she has found a home with a fellow lover of things that may not seem to align—mindfulness, fashion, yoga, art—I know the blog is serving a need. It's allowing those who feel multipassionate to find a common space.

Not ever being one to fit a mold {I mean, I wore a pink belt around my gold grade-school soccer jersey}, it's helpful to connect with others who also feel outside the mold and seek a sacred space to be seen, heard, and appreciated. Fully, *sans* pretense. The writing practice calls for that sort of vulnerability. My hope is that is experienced when one reads *Tranquility du Jour*.

The decade of posts reflects a continued evolution of interests, passions, struggles, and successes. As we mark this anniversary, I'm in a state of writing exploration by attending conferences, taking online classes, and hosting writing gatherings in hope of honing the craft. What started out as an online journal to sprinkle information and inspiration into the world is now morphing into a practice of deepening my writing through storytelling and soul-searching.

This never-ending desire for tranquility has taken me from Costa Rica to Tobago to France to India to Mexico, back to my Oklahoma roots, and across North America on the Tranquility Tour. It's led me to create my own definition of tranquility as *the quality of calm within a full and meaningful life*. I've become the mother of a pug, lost my firstborn four-legged furry son, written three books, been immersed in grieving my Gramma's passing, weathered two surgeries, built businesses, co-launched a non-profit, and finished two master's degrees. The decade has been rich with fodder, and the blog has offered a much-needed respite for reflection. I'm honored that you've come along for the ride.

Inside the Anthology

As I've culled the 3,000+ blog posts for material to include in this *Anthology*, the ongoing struggle to find my own tranquility stares me in the face. The overwhelming feeling of time lack, consistent busyness, and struggles with finding contentment are continual themes. It's as if I'm listening to a warped record spinning the same song over and over again with an occasional shift in inflection.

Have I really lived the past decade with the same ongoing struggle to be in the moment and accept where I am? Yep, it appears so. And my journey to remedy this tug of war is laid out in black and white throughout this book. The good news? Over the past decade I've dabbled in, practiced, and explored numerous techniques to quiet my monkey mind and share many of them in this collection.

While on an acupuncture table whining about overwhelm a few years into self-employment, my therapist said, "Thank goodness you do yoga. Imagine what your life would be like if you didn't." As I lay there with needles sticking out of various meridians, I began to embrace her comment while staying in sync with my breath.

I took it as her way of sharing that my *modus operandi* leaned toward Type A and that without the practice of yoga, this go-go-go mentality would have even more severe results. *God forbid*. Clearly I speak from experience as a fellow tranquility-seeker who struggles with responding versus reacting, balancing being with doing, and performing mundane tasks like cleaning the litter box.

In this *Anthology* you'll find a smattering of favorite posts on eight common themes: my story, yoga, lifestyle, creativity, entrepreneurship, activism, mindfulness, and travel. There's the decision to pursue a social work degree, my history of animal passion tracing back to grade school, lessons in mindfulness, the announcement of new yoga studio locations, a favorite home practice yoga sequence, takeaways from the Tranquility Tour, how the name Tranquil Space came to be, my tranquility timeline, and 100 random things.

My hope is that this project will provide a tangible tool for tranquility *sans* digging through archives. I've carefully chosen photographs featuring simple pleasures of daily life, a peek into my world, and Parisian travels to sprinkle throughout.

In a tradition since *Hip Tranquil Chick*, you'll find a smattering of Savvy Sources, along with *Tranquility du Jour* podcasts aligned with the chapter's topic. This book encapsulates a sampling of the past decade's effort to live tranquilly.

In addition to these updated and enhanced blog favorites, you'll find a muse at the start of each chapter tying a bow around the various posts and offering new insight on how to infuse more tranquility into your every day.

May these stories and essays offer you a peek into a fellow tranquility-seeker's journey in a way that inspires, entertains, and entices into a life of meaning. I'm striving for it and I reckon you are, too.

I hope the workbook nature of this *Anthology* will allow you, too, to reflect, laugh, nod in agreement, and take away a sprinkling of inspirational nuggets. Dog-ear pages that speak to you. Underline passages you'd like to remember. Add comments in the sidebars. Fill out the Takeaways with a colorful pen. Share a page from your book on Twitter using #tdjanthology.

Set this by your bedside. Pick it up when seeking visual or written inspiration. Think of it as a mini memoir from a fellow soul sister desperately seeking tranquility. May we continue to explore it together in the years to come. *Bon anniversaire Tranquility du Jour.*

Bisous, Kimberly

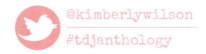

@kimberlywilson
#tdjanthology

facebook.com/tranquilitydujour
instagram.com/tranquilitydujour
youtube.com/tranquilitydujour
tranquilitydujour.com
pinterest.com/kimberlywilson

~ BONJOUR TAKEAWAYS ~

CHAPTER 2:
My Story

And the day came when the risk to remain tight in a bud was more painful that the risk it took to blossom. —Anaïs Nin

Sitting fireside on a pink meditation cushion one chilly October evening in 2004 I began this blogging adventure. My first post was "What are TranquiliT Thoughts" {the blog's name at that time} and here it is:

> As an avid journal writer and a firm believer in creating community, I thought putting together a blog for the Tranquil Space community would be a great way to share ideas about yoga, the practice on AND off the mat: watch for ideas on creating a home practice, ways to create a signature style, figuring out headstand, how to breathe deeper, tips for creating an oasis at home, and all sorts of other lifestyle related tips for living your practice. I will post to the blog as the muse hits. Please check back regularly and feel free to share your thoughts or questions with me at kimberly@tranquilspace.com. Please visit our monthly newsletter for all the updates at Tranquil Space yoga in Dupont Circle, where yoga is not just poses, but a lifestyle.

Although I hadn't read blogs, I kept hearing about them, and blending my passions for journal writing and writing for publication sounded genius. Over the decade, many adventures have unfolded, and I've chosen ten that represented a sampling, such as my return to graduate school, creative dreams, going on semi-sabbatical at the studio, saying goodbye to loved ones, and more. In a way this entire blog is made up of my stories, musings, and confessions, and this chapter is no exception.

While exposing oneself through a blog may not be everyone's cuppa tea, doing so has allowed me to process emotion, capture highlights, share lessons learned, show up for a regular writing practice, and connect with beautiful beings around the world who have found a dose of tranquility within the pages.

Tune into *Tranquility du Jour* podcasts #100, #200, #250 for more insights on my story.

Anthology Extras: Tranquility Timeline
April 2009

Below is a list of highlights and insightful tidbits into the background of how my journey began and continues to unfold, regularly updated with snippets of tranquility. I encourage you to make one too. Explore the highlights that have defined you, made you proud, and shaped who you are. Happy timelining!

June 30, 1973 born in Lawton, Oklahoma as a Midwestern Cancerian.

1981 began journal writing

May 1991 graduated from high school.

May 1995 graduated from University of Oklahoma. Drove to Chicago to see Oprah show and got a Mary Engelbreit sunflower tattooed on my belly.

July—September 1995 backpacked around Europe with money earned while working part-time in college.

October 1995—August 1996 lived in Summit County, Colorado, skiing, snowboarding, selling clothes at DKNY, and working for Keystone Resort. Took first yoga class.

September 1996 drove to D.C. to begin paralegal program at Georgetown University. Worked as a receptionist and got my first email address.

September—November 1997 drove to Alaska from D.C. and down West Coast camping.

December 1997—August 1999 worked as a trademark paralegal at a law firm.

June 1999 took first yoga teacher training.

August 1999 began teaching yoga at a Gold's Gym on Capitol Hill.

October 1999 opened up living room to teach yoga.

January 2000 got nose pierced.

July 2000 took a two-week teacher training in California and plunged into self-employment.

Summer 2000 took course at Women's Business Center. Completed Nia and Pilates training. Offered first Wild Woman Workshop. Started teaching yoga at Joy of Motion.

Fall 2000—May 2003 rented beautiful church parlor space on 16th street.

January 2001 began offering creativity circles.

August 2001 began women's studies master's program at George Washington University.

February 2002 led first international yoga retreat to Costa Rica.

March 2002 offered first teacher training.

May 2002 launched TranquiliT at local lounge with fashion show, yoga demos, and fundraiser. Raised $2,000 for D.C. Rape Crisis Center.

November 2002 found two-level yoga space on P Street.

December 2002 released first yoga CD—*An Intermediate Practice*.

June 2003 moved into home on P Street after numerous bureaucratic delays. Turned 30 in Ibiza, Spain.

October 2003 solidified book idea. Began buying books on writing a proposal and getting published.

December 2003 released second yoga CD—*Vinyasa Yoga for the Newbie Yogi*.

January 2004 began dating Le Beau.

Spring 2004 began designing own tops and additional pants for TranquiliT.

August 2004 finished master's program and bought the Pink Palace.

October 2004 got book agent and started blogging.

December 2004 TranquiliT featured in *Shape* and found Le Pug.

May 2005 Hip Tranquil Chick article featured in *Fit Yoga*, TranquiliT featured in *Washingtonian*, and showed TranquiliT at first yoga conference.

June 2005 spoke at Women's Business Conference on leaving a legacy.

September 2005 launched podcast.

September—December 2005 returned to ballet classes after an 18-year hiatus.

October 2005 signed book contract with Inner Ocean Publishing.

November 2005 featured in book *Starting from Scratch*.

January 2006 took first knitting class.

March 2006 interviewed on *Martha Stewart Living* radio and TranquiliT was featured in *Daily Candy*.

July 2006 co-launched Tranquil Space Foundation.

August 2006 attended Sarah Powers's yin yoga teacher training and Woodhull Ethical Leadership training.

October 2006 took French classes and was worst in class.

November 2006 attended creativity retreat in Mallorca, Spain. Hosted *Hip Tranquil Chick* book launch.

December 2006 released third yoga CD: *Get Your Yoga On*.

April 2007 Tranquil Space named among top 25 yoga studios in the world by *Travel + Leisure*. Took one-month Jivamukti yoga teacher training.

May 2007 donated Jeep to charity and traded for white cruiser bike with pink rims.

July 2007 signed lease on new 4,000 square foot home for Tranquil Space. Nine-month build out began.

September 2007 launched Tranquil Space Arlington.

October 2007 hosted first annual Tranquil Space Foundation gala.

January 2008 launched online creativity circle. Began Authentic Leadership Program at Naropa University.

March 2008 featured in book *Life Entrepreneurs*.

May 2008 opened three-level home in Dupont Circle: three studios, spa, and boutique. Added pink streaks to my tresses. Switched to 100% wind-powered electricity.

~ Reader Feedback ~

I first came upon Kimberly's work in a bookshop in Santa Barbara. I was on a business trip, and having guy troubles, and her book, *Hip Tranquil Chick*, jumped off the shelf and into my hands. I felt that she had written the book especially for me. I devoured it and wanted more. I was thrilled to find out that she had a blog, and a podcast. I was instantly smitten. I started reading the recent entries on the blog, but it wasn't long before I delved into the archives, searching for nuggets on how to bring tranquility into my often frenetic life. Kimberly was the voice of reason in a crazy world. She wasn't advocating an extreme lifestyle. Instead, she offered her own learning path, sharing her steps and stumbles, leaps and hops along the way.

As I read through the archives, I started to learn a little more about marrying my sparkling princess self to my granola yogini. Until then, I thought I needed to choose one over the other. Kimberly was my inspiration. Each day, I would read about her daily adventures and life lessons, and each day, I was inspired. I signed up for an Authentic Leadership course at Naropa University based on Kimberly's recommendations. I found myself embracing palazzo pants, wraps, and bed days. I no longer felt guilty about being drawn to pretty things, but I turned down the dial on acquiring too many of them. I've been a crafter for many years, and loved when Kimberly shared her own crafting adventures, reminding us that handmade items are priceless.

Over the years, I've been lucky enough to take an online course and meet Kimberly as part of her Tranquility Tour. I understood just how authentic Kimberly's voice was. Meeting her made me realize that in this world of social media phoniness, celebrity worship, and the pursuit of materialism, authenticity still exists. But it's rare. I've sneaked peeks at her blog when I'm in boring meetings, used her packing lists to help me on my European excursions, laughed at the antics of her pets that are so similar to mine, and followed her learning path as I have embraced my own. In doing so, I am reminded daily that we should embrace the process and the journey, and not just seek the destination.

Melanie Feeny, Utah

June 2008 solo sojourn for 15 hours in New York City in celebration of my 35th: practiced yoga, sipped rose tea, ate cupcakes, dined on organic cuisine, and browsed bookstores.

July 2008 met with team at New World Library. Began writing second book, *Tranquilista*.

August 2008 opened TranquiliT showroom and taught at Kripalu.

September 2008 featured in *Washington Times*. Began offering contemplative crafting classes at TranquiliT showroom.

October 2008 began tweeting {@tranquilista}. Honored as a new leader in philanthropy by Greater D.C. Cares.

November 2008 featured designer on washingtonian.com and showed TranquiliT at Green Festival.

January 2009 attended inaugural ball donning TranquiliT armwarmers. Started boxing with pink gloves.

February 2009 signed up for creative non-fiction writing classes. Mentioned in *U.S. News* as celebrity-style coach.

September 2009 returned to graduate school to pursue a master's in social work.

October 2009 celebrated 10 years of Tranquil Space.

November 2009 took 10 days to bask in Paris.

January 2010 took first art journaling course in Mexico. *Tranquilista* hit shelves.

February 2010 hosted *Tranquilista* book launch *fête*.

March 2010 West Coast book tour.

April 2010 TranquiliT named "Eco-Chic Rising Star" by Fashion Group International.

June 2010 West Coast book tour part two.

August 2010 Texas book tour.

November 2010 journeyed to India and fell in love with a street dog nicknamed Lumpy-ji.

January 2011 hosted India Night Benefit to raise money for animal and environmental non-profits in India.

March 2011 named among top four yoga teachers in D.C. by *Washingtonian* magazine.

April 2011 completed 400-hour internship at N Street Village.

June 2011 joined board of Pigs Animal Sanctuary. Featured in *Transforming Scholarship*.

July 2011 hosted Benefit for the Animals to celebrate Farm Sanctuary's 25th anniversary, humane education of Washington Humane Society, and Pigs Animal Sanctuary.

August 2011 attended Disney's Leadership Institute.

September 2011 attended Farm Sanctuary's Animal Care Conference.

October 2011 hosted first Art + Yoga retreat in West Virginia. Sponsored and attended Farm Sanctuary's End Factory Farming conference.

January 2012 launched *Tranquilologie* e-course. Spent a week art journaling in Mexico.

February 2012 said goodbye to beloved Gramma and began deep mourning process.

May 2012 began semi-sabbatical and headed to France to host two 10-day retreats.

July 2012 attended the World Domination Summit in Portland. Hosted Tranquility Summer Camp.

August 2012 attended two animal rights conferences. Released 250th podcast.

September 2012 released a limited edition art journal toolkit. Hosted Pigs Animal Santuary's 20th-year anniversary *fête*.

November 2012 returned to India to immerse in yoga.

December 2012 released *Tranquility du Jour Daybook*.

January 2013 unveiled new website. Began eight-week mindfulness-based stress reduction course.

April 2013 completed 600-hour internship at Amtrak. Announced the Tranquility Tour.

May 2013 received master's degree in social work. Went on silent meditation retreat.

June 2013 turned 40 in Paris.

July 2013 attended the World Domination Summit in Portland. Lost my beloved baby kitty Bonnard.

August 2013 co-hosted parents' 50th anniversary party. Attended Victoria Moran's Vegan Academy.

September 2013 hosted Tranquility Tour kick-off and *Tranquilologie* release. Set off on two-month Tranquility Tour adventure.

December 2013 hosted Tranquility Tour tea for 300th podcast. Released *Tranquility du Jour Daybook* 2.0. Adopted rescue kitten Jackson Cezanne.

January 2014 Celebrated 10 years with Le Beau.

March 2014 completed Mindful Schools weekend training.

May 2014 co-hosted Art + Asana Costa Rica retreat with Mary Catherine Starr. Took documentary filmmaking classes.

June 2014 attended seven-day mindfulness-based stress reduction training with Jon Kabat-Zinn and returned to Paris to write.

1. NEXT ON THE HORIZON
May 2009

Considering the ample relfection and social time I'm blessed with in Costa Rica, I am feeling good about a next step on the horizon. For years I've debated a master's in social work {MSW}. Actually, it's what I set out to do in university {psych major, soc minor} so the idea continues to beckon *moi*. In 2004 I completed my master's in women's studies and loved the exploration of feminism on a deep level.

Recently I find myself running into women I admire who have MSWs overseeing non-profits or doing therapy. I think it is a sign. To top it off, while swinging in the hammocks discussing existentialism with a fellow retreater yesterday, I decided this was my next step. And I think she's joining me on the journey, too.

Just broke the news to Le Beau and look forward to exploring it further when I'm home. This past decade has been an organic evolution building Tranquil Space. Lord knows I'm not done with this journey, but have been pondering what the next decade will present for *moi*. I believe I've found it. The chance to continue trying to make a difference in this new way thrills me.

Now that I've determined what the next decade holds, I must dine on papaya, pineapple, watermelon, granola, and fresh juice before strolling through the coffee fields and teaching yoga.

> The chance to continue trying to make a difference in this new way thrills me.

2. CREATIVE DREAMS
July 2009

Monday night I hosted a creativity gathering in the TranquiliT showroom. I was joined by a lovely group of ladies who explored their creative dreams, engaged in free writing, encouraged one another, learned my top five tips for creative flair . . . while sipping bubbly and noshing on brie. It was a delightful evening and I, too, came away inspired from their energy. Yay for creative dreams!

One of my favorite books that addresses creative dreams is SARK's *Make Your Creative Dreams Real* {tune into *Tranquility du Jour* podcasts #122 and #205}. A fun, colorful read. What are your creative dreams? What small steps can you take TODAY to move toward making them a reality?

Here is a potpourri of my creative dreams:

- Tranquil Teens nationwide
- MSW
- PhD
- Teach yoga to prisoners
- Therapist in private practice focused on supporting and empowering women
- Tiny studio flat in New York and/or Paris
- Quaint stand-alone TranquiliT shoppe
- Handmade TranquiliT by *moi*
- Return to beading one-of-a-kind necklaces
- Write a best-seller and have a fun book tour to meet oodles of interesting ladies
- Have a potbelly pig as a pet {or two}
- Create a fragrance
- Win a grant from Eileen Fisher or Martha Stewart
- Plant a larger garden
- Host a talk show/TV lifestyle segment
- Run businesses slated among the top 100 small biz to work in

Now to slumber and dream of pink, sparkly Parisian apartments.

Anthology Extras: 100 Things
May 2010

Originally I planned to only do 50, then I got to 60, then 75 and kept going. This was fun. And I'd love to see what comes up for you with this exercise.

1. I'm from the Great Plains... Oklahoma.

2. I just read Ted Leonsis's book *The Business of Happiness* and want to create a list of 101 things I want to do in this lifetime.

3. The "old man grunts" Le Pug makes brings me joy.

4. My favorite restaurant is the Olive Garden. I know, I know.

5. I love to plant impatiens each spring.

6. Zen by Tazo green tea with agave nectar is my every-morning go-to.

7. I'm currently obsessed with setting up the perfect Pink Palace creative space.

8. I will finish my MSW in 2013 and plan to add therapy to my offerings and focus on expanding my non-profit Tranquil Space Foundation.

9. I'm a bath junkie—some days I take two LUSH-filled baths.

10. *J'adore* mind mapping—this is how I outlined *Tranquilista*.

11. I heart Air Supply and have a penchant for really bad music.

12. Potbelly pigs kill me—in a good way. I want my own someday.

13. I have dreams of sewing, beading, writing, and creating full time.

14. I now have my first gifted bottle of Chanel perfume in my possession.

15. I'm an INFJ—introvert at heart who needs oodles of alone time.

16. I believe the answers to life's questions can be found in books.

17. Reading without a pen is impossible for me—I *must* underline.

18. I prefer simple milk chocolate over fancy dark chocolate.

19. My every-so-often indulgence is a soy chai latte at Starbucks.

20. I used to sit on the fence and tell "super cow" stories to the cows at my grandparents' farm.

21. After college I backpacked through Europe for three months.

22. Peonies are my favorite floral indulgence.

23. The smell of fresh-baked chocolate chip cookies is a gift from God.

24. My sweet tooth rules my life.

25. I created Tranquil Space to serve as a community for like-hearted Washingtonians to do yoga and sip tea.

26. I am overly sensitive in many ways—even to noise and bright lights.

27. My dosha is *Vata-Pitta*.

28. I was recently gifted a beautiful antique jewelry box embellished with buttons on top and the word "passion" inside.

29. Statistics {math in general} makes me cry.

30. Flying has become intensely anxiety-producing.

31. I was a ballerina in grade school and junior high.

32. I was the co-captain of our high school Pom Pom team but never understood {nor was interested} in the silly football and basketball games where we danced.

33. I tried soccer in grade school, cried each time the ball came at

me, and wore a pink skinny belt over my jersey.

34. Leading Tranquil Teens programs to receptive teenage girls brings me great pleasure.

35. I long to be an inspiring leader to my studio and non-profit's teams.

36. Sitting still is very challenging for me.

37. I love to wear and design with layers.

38. My hobbies {and my babies} are my businesses.

39. I have questionable parenting skills based on the behavior/personality disorders of my three pets.

40. My kitchen is wasted space—need more bookshelves.

41. I'm a vegetarian with strong cravings for fried chicken.

42. *J'adore* pink, pink, and more pink.

43. I've worn mostly all black since 2006. No reason. Just because.

44. I like the beach except that gritty sand is irritating and vast water scares me.

45. I prefer car camping.

46. I beg Le Beau to rent an RV to drive *moi* and Le Pug cross-country.

47. I'm addicted to my Planner Pad.

48. I believe it's not a party unless there is a gift bag and tons of scented candles.

49. *J'adore* donning pink boxing gloves and hitting my 70lb pink heavy bag.

50. Yoga is my sustenance.

51. Rarely watch TV but, when I do, it often involves true crime.

52. Meditation is an ongoing daily goal. Started today with 10 minutes of it and feel great.

53. I long to have my own Etsy store.

54. Nag champa incense is dreamy and lit nightly in the Pink Palace.

55. My heart belonged to my grandpa who died of lung cancer when I was six.

56. I've never smoked a cigarette.

57. I enjoy smoking a cigar on special occasions.

58. I have a master's in women's studies from George Washington University.

59. I'd like a PhD in women's studies or something equally interesting.

60. I enjoy doing TV interviews, interviewing on my podcast, and hosting e-courses. Connecting brings me great pleasure.

61. I only read non-fiction—business or self-help or memoir or creativity.

> Today I tweeted the mantra "ponder what seeds you're planting, what needs watering, and what needs weeding."
>
> Consider:
>
> **1. What seeds are you currently planting?**
> *Moi*: education/professional development
>
> **2. What needs watering?**
> *Moi*: personal relationships, down time, crafty/creative time, studying time
>
> **3. What needs weeding?**
> *Moi*: clutter—mental and physical

62. My design esthetic is Zen Princess.

63. I've had to make many hard decisions over the past 10.5 years as a business owner.

64. Journal writing is my outlet.

65. I'm currently obsessed with visual journaling.

66. I desperately want to immerse myself in mixed media play.

67. I LOVE making inspiration boards on manila file folders.

68. I believe Paris, Venice, and New York City offer oodles of inspiration.

69. I wish to spend time making art, making magic, and making a difference.

70. Beyond grateful for my supportive Le Beau, loving parents, and feisty 98-year-old Gramma.

71. I heart cucumber rolls and miso soup.

72. I despise clutter, but often find myself surrounded by self-induced clutter.

73. I was obsessed with turtles growing up and had Myrtle, Urtle, Yurtle, Nosy and Pudding who were all eventually buried in my backyard.

74. I used to color my hair with peroxide and a hair dryer in junior high.

75. I'll be at *Sex and the City 2* on opening day and now want to travel to Morocco.

76. I've always been curious on deep levels about the meaning of life and how to live it with no regrets.

77. My journey to becoming a therapist has been circuitous.

78. I have zip, nada, no business training.

79. I run my organizations based on intuition, book knowledge, and a focus on what I would want as a consumer.

80. I think rats are cute and don't understand why others are scared of them.

81. I grew up with hamsters, newts, and garter snakes as pets.

82. Gossip makes me sad.

83. Cruelty to animals breaks my heart.

84. I'm beyond excited to go to India later this year.

85. I see a spiritual pilgrimage of sort in my future.

86. In junior high I was a born-again Christian who carried my bible to school {wrapped in pretty paper, of course}.

87. I cried when I realized I couldn't be perfect and was too much of a sinner.

88. I'm drawn to Buddhism and can't get enough of this compassionate philosophy.

89. I love shipping TranquiliT orders—it's like sending gifts every day.

90. Accessories bring me great joy.

91. I picture myself traveling and using my skill set in big ways as I age—think Audrey Hepburn and UNICEF.

92. I constantly struggle with time management and crave constant efficiency.

93. B+s break my heart—too close to the golden A.

94. Muir Woods is one of my favorite places on earth.

95. In 1996 I drove from D.C. to Alaska and down the West Coast for three months.

96. I felt liberated when told that I didn't need to seek work/life balance because they were so intertwined.

97. I am currently addicted to green smoothies and orange cheese with chives.

98. I am inspired by Melinda Gates, Madonna, Martha Stewart, Sharon Gannon, Amy Butler, and Steve Jobs . . . to name a few.

99. I bought a harmonium in 2008 and still have yet to learn it.

100. I love cotton candy—the smell, taste, and texture.

1.
2.
3.
4.
5.
6.
7.
8.
9.
10.
11.
12.
13.
14.
15.
16.
17.
18.
19.
20.
21.
22.
23.
24.
25.

Use the following pages to create your own list.

26.
27.
28.
29.
30.
31.
32.
33.
34.
35.
36.
37.
38.
39.
40.
41.
42.
43.
44.
45.
46.
47.
48.
49.
50.

51.
52.
53.
54.
55.
56.
57.
58.
59.
60.
61.
62.
63.
64.
65.
66.
67.
68.
69.
70.
71.
72.
73.
74.
75.

76.
77.
78.
79.
80.
81.
82.
83.
84.
85.
86.
87.
88.
89.
90.
91.
92.
93.
94.
95.
96.
97.
98.
99.
100.

3. TWO MONTHS POST-SURGERY
May 2010

I'm writing this while sitting outside a Starbucks on Tuesday night sipping Tazo Calm tea. Dreamy. I think it is safe to say that I have never been able to enjoy a sidewalk café on a Tuesday night or, honestly, on most weeknights over the past decade. If I'm not teaching, I've usually been in some sort of meeting so I'm feeling incredibly decadent at the moment. Yay for summer school forcing me to shake things up!

I wanted to take a step back to honor this tiny two-month shoulder surgery anniversary. It's been an interesting ride. I have about 50% range of movement, am in ongoing discomfort, have a tightened capsule around the joint {whatever that means}, lack the ability to move my right arm on its own fully, and continue with physical therapy two+ hours per week. Torn rotator cuffs and bone spurs aren't too sexy. Tomorrow I'll see the surgeon and get feedback on my progress.

Being without yoga for two months has been a challenging adjustment. At first my body ached from lack of vinyasas; now it's gotten used to being lethargic and prefers sitting to movement of any kind. Uh oh. I have one month left *sans* yoga or boxing and I know my return to the mat will be more than humbling. Ironically, I'll have thumb surgery in July and be in a cast for six weeks. Talk about lessons in detachment.

Once fall rolls around I should be injury-free and ready to rock my regular, beloved, and oh-so-needed yoga practice. These past eight weeks have served up many lessons and reminders. Here are a few:

1. **Yoga is important**: It's an emotional, mental, physical, and spiritual outlet for *moi*.

2. **Honor the small steps**: Stopping pain pills three days after surgery, getting around *sans* sling, sleeping *sans* swath, lifting a cane in physical therapy.

3. **When life throws you challenges, make 'em sparkle**: I added a sparkly cover to my swath and rocked it for weeks.

4. **Lighten your load**: Having two overstuffed bags in tow at all times is too much. I try to carry only essentials now and my shoulders seem grateful.

5. **Get comfortable saying "sorry, I can't"**: I've had to bow out of many opportunities that would have overstuffed an already full calendar or challenged a body in repair.

6. **Honor your energy**: In the past when I'd come home from a long work day I'd open the computer and work until the wee hours handling emails, projects, online orders. Now I find myself saying "it'll have to wait until tomorrow, I'm pooped!" and it feels good.

7. **Savor the slow down**: Life came to a slow halt for the first few weeks as I struggled to use my right side again. This helped me smell the flowers along the way and to add time to my usual tasks.

8. **Think big picture**: These eight weeks are a snippet in my life journey. I'm doing my best to move through these short term struggles to have long-term gain.

May these injuries continue to teach me lessons and may I embrace them with a compassionate heart. This experience can only enhance my teaching and my empathy for others' suffering and physical challenges. *Ommm*.

4. NEW INK
May 2011

I'm back from two days of train travel to and from Montreal, three days in Montreal and a day in NYC. Arrived home this morning around 3:30 a.m. Have oodles of photos and adventures to share, but am about to crawl into bed before an early trip to Oklahoma tomorrow morning. Family time, here I come {with a pug in a pink bag, of course}.

I've been contemplating a second tattoo. I wanted to wait until I was 100% sure, through with comps {which I passed with a 91.5%}, and feeling a bit lighter in my load. This time away felt perfect, and it was spontaneous. I opted for the Sanskrit version of my favorite mantra, *Lokah Samastah Sukhino Bhavantu*, as cursive English wouldn't fit on one line.

I donned sunnies to block out the overhead lights and make the experience, well, more tranquil. A lavender eyepillow, cup of chamomile tea, and nag champa incense would have been even better.

We stayed at the rockstar Hotel Chelsea {*sans* bathroom in room} so I chose next door's Chelsea Tattoo Company. Hip-hop and punk music played loudly in the background. I requested Air Supply but the artist was unfamiliar with my fave old school band. I know, I know, but I heart *Lost in Love*. Don't you?

Was it painful? Insanely so, but super quick. Considering last year's surgeries where pain lingers for months, this was much easier {but anesthesia would have been accepted}. It was throbbing for a couple of hours afterwards but feels good as new now. The process took 45 minutes to an hour and I was squeezing Le Beau's hand most of the time while doing lion's breath, and occasionally squealing. For which I was shushed by my artist. When I left I had red lipstick all over my mouth from all the lion's breaths—not pretty.

Happy with my new ink. It marks the halfway point in my MSW program, comps congrats, and a continuous reminder of: *May all beings everywhere be happy and free. May the thoughts, words, and actions of my own life contribute in some way to that happiness and to that freedom for all.* Love!

5. GRAMMA IS AN ANGEL
February 2012

I headed to Texas on Friday for a weekend of Gramma cuddles. Nothing could have prepared me for what was to come. I feel as if I've been through some sort of war.

Today is my first "normal" day in almost a week. I will eat, shower, and head to school—some semblance of a routine. The past few days have been a whirlwind filled with tears, hand holding, and extreme pain.

On Saturday Gramma took a decline and I called repeatedly for nurses. The hospice nurse said she had only a few days left and I was crushed. My Gramma's only words were "thank you dear" when I told her how beautiful she was. Mom and I stayed with her for 10 hours on Saturday. We stayed all day Sunday, and slept there with her. Monday we took turns leaving to shower and recoup. Monday night at 10:30

p.m., she took her last breath. I honestly don't know if I'll ever be the same. She was truly my favorite person ever.

There are five stages of grief, and I have yet to fully move through any. Looks like I've got a long way to go. Oh, and below is her obituary, which sheds some light on what a remarkable woman she was. Truly.

~~~

Lillian Myrtle Stotlar Ewing Couch, age 99, was born September 17, 1912 in Devils Lake, ND to Nelle Reid Stotlar and Bert A. Stotlar, and died February 20, 2012.

Lillian graduated from North Dakota State University in 1935 and married Elmer Leigh Ewing the following year on the day of his graduation from NDSU in Fargo, ND. They lived for many years in Lawton and Midwest City, Oklahoma, where both were teachers. She taught at Lincoln Elementary School and was the first Lawton teacher to integrate by teaching the 3rd grade at Douglas Elementary School. In 1966 they moved to Midwest City as a teaching team and she taught at Rose Elementary School. Together they traveled the world after retirement, returning to their home at Lake Fort Cobb, Oklahoma until Elmer's death in 1980.

In 1982, she married Orval Bradley Couch and moved to his home in Homer, LA. They traveled extensively in their Airstream and with tour groups until his death in 2000. While in Homer she was active in the Country Club and Garden Club. Lillian moved to Wichita Falls, TX to be nearer to her children in 2006 and resided at Rolling Meadows; then at The Gables.

She was active in the Methodist Church in every community in which she lived over the years. She served as Wesleyan Guild president, in state offices as well, was sponsor for youth groups and was always a favorite chaperone for both Camp Fire Girls groups and Methodist Youth Fellowship groups. She taught crafts and archery at Camp Fire camps, and assisted with Cub Scouts and PTA groups. She lived an admirable and valuable life.

~~~

I left Texas Tuesday evening and listened to loud hip-hop for hours. It seemed to be the only thing that helped stop the tears. Yesterday I was in bed most of the day resting—except for a massage and a practice of legs up the wall in my gym's steam room. My poor body is a mess with all sorts of tweaks due to lack of movement, grief, and travel over the past week. Yoga and mindfulness practice came in incredibly handy during Gramma's final days. I was able to sit with her, hold her hands, massage her forehead and arms, and be fully present. Despite my typical tendency to multitask, I transitioned into a new state of awareness with her and credit it all to yoga.

Le Beau, Le Pug, and *moi* are driving to Oklahoma on Friday for her Monday memorial. It's a 22-hour drive and Le Beau is up for the challenge.

I'm so grateful for the numerous love notes posted on my Facebook wall and appreciate the outpouring of support during this time. Please consider dedicating your next practice to her, wish her well on this new journey, or send my family love. It will be well-received.

> Despite my typical tendency to multitask, I transitioned into a new state of awareness with her and credit it all to yoga.

6. TRANSITIONS
March 2012

Bonjour, my lovelies. This week began with a boom. Monday {the day Gramma died} is always hard and the one-month anniversary of Gramma's death {Tuesday} left me incapacitated. I slowly rebounded the next day, but waves of grief are oddly fascinating and I feel like I'm riding an emotional roller coaster *sans* squeals of glee. I'm learning to ride them as best I can while gratefully realizing that each and every day is different. I purchased *Grieving Mindfully: A Compassionate and Spiritual Guide to Dealing with Loss* by Sameet Kumar and look forward to diving into it this weekend. Seemed right up my alley.

> If we don't change, we don't grow. If we don't grow, we aren't really living.
> —Gail Sheehy

I've been pondering some sort of transition and alluded to it in my Week in Reviews. I know my final year of graduate school will be challenging due to a 20-hour internship at Amtrak's Employee Assistance Program, four final classes, and various endeavors. With the passing of my Gramma, I've been pushed toward a transition. A move I *knew* I must make. I need time and space to mourn, process the grief, and prepare for my intense final year of graduate school. Thus, I've decided to take a semi-sabbatical from my day-to-day efforts at Tranquil Space {my baby of nearly 13 years} and I sent the team a memo today. Here are snippets of it:

Dearest Team: I'm writing to update you on an important upcoming change at Tranquil Space "world headquarters." Effective May 15, 2012 I will be taking a semi-sabbatical and slowly phasing out my day-to-day over the next 7 weeks. Since starting this seedling in my living room nearly 13 years ago, I've found myself eating, sleeping, and breathing this beloved baby. Plus I have also been nurturing new "babies"—TranquiliT, books, Tranquil Space Foundation, podcast/blog, Tranquil Space Arlington, and my latest grad program—at the same time.

You'll still find me teaching my regular classes and offerings during my semi-sabbatical plus working on creative and strategic measures for Tranquil Space behind the scenes. I believe it is good for business owners to take a step back, build on successes, and brainstorm fresh ideas.

Thank you for your support during this time of bereavement and for being the most amazing cOMmunity ever. I am honored to be able to work with such a talented, thoughtful team.

It was so hard to hit send. Made it oddly real and almost surreal. I felt it deep inside my heart and belly. Many beloved team members have proclaimed that this is long overdue.

Today's non-profit management guest teacher spoke about staff development. She emphasized the importance of self-care for managers and stated, "You need to bring your A game to the office every day." A light bulb went off. *That* is my problem right now. I can't bring my A game to anything at the moment and it's an indication that I need to regroup and focus on self-care.

What are the chances that a guest teacher would offer such insights moments after I send a memo? Synchronicity at work. Moments of tranquilosophy. Anyone else dabbling in the experience of transition? It's scary, gut wrenching, empowering, and exhilarating all rolled into one. Sending transitional love your way.

7. SNOWED-IN REFLECTIONS
December 2012

I hope you are savoring some downtime after the holiday hubbub. Today began with a Boxing Day agenda and sly plans to beat the storm. As we pulled out of the driveway, we promptly turned around and decided not to venture into the unknown. The road was already slick and the snow had just begun. Throughout the day I watched it fall with stars in my eyes while also recalculating lots of plans.

We worked late at the studio and dashed to the woods on Christmas Eve, while snow poured from the sky. We made plans to stock up today. No luck. Random smatterings of fruit, veggies, and canned soups it is!

Also, had big plans to get Le Chat Bonnard into a kitty internist tomorrow to identify the mass in front of his heart, but had to reschedule as we're not going anywhere. For awhile.

The snow fell {six to eight inches}, turned to sleet, and finally stopped around dusk. The woods are quiet, oh-so-white, and not allowing us to escape. Honestly, I'm ok with that.

Le Beau has tinkered with new bike toys all day while I finished reading Phillip Moffitt's latest book, *Emotional Chaos to Clarity* {highly recommend}, filled in my new *Tranquility du Jour Daybook* with a pink marker, penned thoughts in my journal, chased sticks in the snow with Le Pug, sat fireside, and did what I do best . . . plan.

While looking over the list of things I wanted to handle during the hollydaze, I became disenchanted with how slowly items were getting checked off, and by how I'd be back to internship and school before I knew it—without completion. I only have a few days left as next week I'm in NYC to study with my Jivamukti

teachers and to hear activists Jenny Brown of Woodstock Animal Sanctuary and Julia Butterfly Hill speak. Then, it's back to life for my final semester of graduate school.

So here's my holiday wish list: strategic plans for businesses, daily exercise, Facetime crochet dates with Mama Wilson {damn those granny squares}, record *Daybook* video, *Tranquilologie* edits, 2012 year in review, 2013 dreams, sign up for Vegan Academy, fill in 2013 *Daybook*, pen newsletter, go through magazines, pen and mail heaps of thank yous, clear out inbox, special *Tranquilologie* podcast for subscribers, finish sketchbook.

Dear lord. Where's the breather? While reading Phillip's book, he talked about "ordinary compulsion" defined as "a reactive state of mind that interferes with the natural flow and rhythm of your life. It can prevent you from acting with your deepest intentions and deprive you of genuine choices. Ordinary compulsion can interfere with getting things done or prevent you from letting go of a disappointment."

Hmmm. I've diagnosed myself with an ordinary compulsion to plan and note what hasn't yet been done {and may not get done this holiday season, *ommmm*, let it go} to the detriment of savoring the present moment. In yoga these conditioned patterns are coined *samskaras*. All day I felt resistance toward wanting to simply sit and read versus figure out my life in 2013. It was a powerful, emotionally charged tug of war.

I'm emerging without too many battle wounds this evening. I share my struggle wondering if you, too, experience this internal conflict between busyness and spaciousness. Doing and being. It's an ongoing journey, and I hope to be more gentle with myself in the New Year. Plan, set goals, and embrace more self-care while reconfiguring *samskaras* into more mindful pursuits. Wanna join *moi*?

Anthology Extras: One Year of Le Pug
December 2005

Today marks an official year of having little Le Pug in my life. What a year it has been since we picked him up from his family in Springwater, NY. We had a choice between him or the pick of the litter. I had read to avoid picking a puppy with a runny nose or any signs of breathing issues.

As soon as I scooped him up, he sneezed in my face, and I knew I had to have him over the so-called *crème de la crème*. To me, Le Pug is the pick of the universe! This dog has brought more joy to our lives than I could ever imagine. He's hard to control when he gets excited, loves to lick and sneeze, eats everything in sight, and wakes me up every morning between 1-4 a.m. for his breakfast. However, I can't remember life before him as he's become so ingrained in our lives. A few lessons that Le Pug has taught, and continues to teach, me:

1. **Every day is exciting**. He never wakes up in a bad mood as each day is a new adventure for our canine companion. Imagine bolting out of bed every morning excited about what the day will hold.

2. **A little love goes a long way**. Le Pug is never short on affection. He wants to be involved in everything we do, appears content just to be in our presence, and asks for very little in return {except constant attention}. Douse those you care about with attention and care.

3. **Ask for what you want**. Sure 3 a.m. breakfast may seem insane, but you'll never know if you don't ask. Be bold and request what you need.

4. **Take naps.** When the going gets tough, Le Pug gets sleepy. A little self-care goes a long way for all of us.

5. **Mark your territory**. Ok, so we all know what I'm referring to here. However, we can take it a step beyond the male dog definition and work to carve out a niche for our lives. How can we leave our mark on the world?

May we have many more years of lessons learned from this wheezing, sniffly, non-pick of the litter.

8. BYE BYE BABY BONNARD
July 2013

I was sipping chai after a meditation class one fall evening when a woman mentioned that she had alley kittens free to a good home. A light bulb went off. I was fresh out of a most dysfunctional relationship and realized the only thing I missed about it was touch. A kitty could easily fix that! We exchanged numbers and I showed up at her home with only love. Yep, no cat carrier. Didn't even have a litter box or kitty food yet. I was a well-intentioned novice.

I got to choose between a tiny white kitty that seemed, well, normal . . . or a feisty black kitty that, frankly, didn't. The black kitty it was. I stuffed him into a cardboard box with air holes and I took him to the nearest big box store to pick up supplies. I immediately knew he was special as he shoved his head through the holes, at times getting stuck.

We developed a beautiful bond that included mid-day messages left for him on my answering machine, a pink floral collar and leash to "walk" him around the 'hood {most emasculating}, and his first rush to the emergency vet the following month for eating something quite intimate that, well, he really shouldn't have.

After getting him neutered, I asked if I could visit him in the hospital. Apparently the vet thought that was odd, then called for back-up when my kitty was too ornery for one person to manage.

He chased people into closets, got riled up if he thought I was being harmed, and would sometimes slap at or bite your calf through the shower curtain when he wanted attention. Bonnard was a staple in the early days of Tranquil Space in my living room. Pulling people's hair with his teeth while they were in *savasana*, getting onto their mats and not moving, and standing in the center of the room during parties, often hissing.

Years went on and Bonnard continued to be alpha, required more vet visits for various health issues, and become quite obese. He was literally OCD about food. When the vet informed me that he was the equivalent of a 400-lb man, I was horrified. However, not having food out 24/7 meant Bonnard would paw at books near my head, pulling them off the shelf—one by one—until I woke up and put more food in the bowl. He was not a fan of an empty bowl. I often found food from kitchen cabinets stashed under my bed or in secret hiding places. Yes, he'd open kitchen cabinets with his paws and pull food to safety.

At one point in 2005, he became blind and partially paralyzed, was failing fast, and was rushed to a kitty neurologist. After a CT scan, a few grand, and some steroids, he made a miraculous recovery. Baffled the vets.

My 33rd birthday was spent visiting Bonnard in the hospital after having two rubber bands extracted from his belly. When we picked him up, he crawled onto Le Beau's lap and pooped while Le Beau drove us all home. No respect. Oh, and this was not new behavior. He peed on an old boyfriend's lap while driving in 2000. He had a thing for sharing his feelings in not-so-subtle ways.

Despite his lack of love for others, he had a thing for me. When my Gramma died, I spent days in bed crying, and he would come to comfort me while Le Pug preferred snoring at the foot of the bed. He slowly grew to tolerate Le Beau and maybe even like him a bit. When pulling together photos of him, I came across many of Bonnard snuggling up to Le Beau who looked fearful. When we first began dating, Bonnard was on the back of the couch and when Le Beau turned around, Bonnard popped him in the forehead. Not yet a fan.

Feisty, yet fabulous.

Bonnard mellowed in his older years, but continued to have numerous health scares, such as the random irritation on his leg that, when healed, grew back with white hair on his all-black frame. His ongoing battle with crystals in his bladder required a special prescription diet from a young age. His occasional need for an electrolyte-filled IV, just because. After a dose of it, he'd perk right back up. And then there was his bout of psychogenic alopecia where he over-groomed his belly, leaving himself half-naked. Oh, and his ongoing need for medication—which we doused in spray cheese for happy consumption.

The decline began October 2012 when he was diagnosed with hyperthyroidism. We planned to go through the radioactive treatment that had a huge success rate, but when the chest x-ray was done in the prep stages, they found fluid there. I was in India so sweet Le Beau had to go through this process solo, count his kitty breaths, and take him to his typically cat-free cabin for monitoring over Thanksgiving. God bless.

> He had a thing for sharing his feelings in not-so-subtle ways.

After surgical extraction of fluids, I had him see a kitty cardiologist to try to identify the cause of the fluid. A mass was found. I still didn't think cancer and was like, "of course he has a mass in front of his kitty heart. I mean, it's Bonnard!" Next stop was an internist in January who told me it was cancer. When he did the sonogram he said neither chemo nor surgery were an option because it was intertwined with organs. He said he'd go this year. My heart broke.

After an April emergency vet visit, we were told he was in hospice care. Although I've slowly been preparing for this moment since his January diagnosis, I still wasn't ready. Over the past week he seemed to be declining rapidly, and on Thursday I contacted my holistic vet to make a Saturday appointment. Friday, I baked all day with a friend in prep for a Tranquil Space teacher tea and secretly felt it was a sweet send-off for my baby. He savored organic whipping crème during the process, followed us around constantly, and chose to spend time in the bathtub most of the party. Some long-time teachers said their goodbyes privately.

Saturday, I took Le Pug to daycare, and spent the day giving Bonnard oodles of treats, hours of stroking, and lots of love. It was hard watching the clock and knowing that there were only so many hours left with him. The vet arrived shortly after 7:15 p.m. It was the hardest thing I'd ever done. That evening, among tears, I purchased the perfect urn for him online, and found Rainbow Bridge {a pet loss grief support community} when Googling "how to grieve pet loss" and "do cats go to heaven." Tonight there is a ceremony tribute, and *moi*, Mama Wilson, and Le Beau will be lighting a candle for Bonnard.

I'm sad he won't be joining us in person on the Tranquility Tour this fall but he definitely will be there in spirit. He seemed a fan of our vintage camper, Miss Lillie, and enjoyed car rides {except when Le Beau got a new car and he crawled into the back seat to puke and poo on it}.

My heart hurts, and although I know it will heal, the pain of loss is still so raw.

When he was a kitten, he came leaping across my living room and knocked Gramma's glasses off her head, leaving them dangling and disfigured. Naturally, I showered her with his photos for years as a reminder of their tormented love.

Ah, the stories could go on and on, but I must get up and pretend to have some sense of normalcy today. Thank you for indulging me and please send lots of love to his sweet spirit that can never be replaced. *Au revoir*, baby Bonnard. You were a true gift. One of a kind.

9. RELATIONSHIPS
January 2014

Woo-hoo today is the official 10-year anniversary of my first date with Le Beau. I got excited and announced it yesterday online but the 22nd is the real deal. Hard to believe I sipped bubbly {him, two beers} one cold January night a decade ago, and we clicked.

We met online {a bit *risqué* in those days}, only to discover that we lived across the street —and worked within two blocks—of each other! We shared a similarly odd sense of humor and wanderlust. And I believe that odd sense of humor is a secret to our longevity.

As a former serial one- to two-year relationship girl, getting past the two-year mark has been, well, eventful. I mean, I've spent 1/4 of my life with this guy, we have three "sons," and run a business and non-profit together. He left his non-profit attorney world to join the Tranquil Space team six years ago and somehow we've made that work. Yes, I'm his boss {although he requested no more annual reviews}, which has its own set of perks and challenges.

Honestly, I credit our longevity to him. He's the adult. The patient one. When I throw a tantrum exclaiming, "I'm done talking!" and climb into the back of the camper with crossed arms to pout {as may have happened once on Tranquility Tour}, he reasons with me as only a mature individual can {I admit, not my finest moment of mindful communication}.

He tolerates more than is imaginable. From living in a tiny pink home with white furniture and three black-haired pets, to holding a funeral for a goldfish in the backyard {when his law school buddies were in town}, to visiting pig sanctuaries and withstanding demands of adopting our own despite loving bacon, to driving my bum 11,500 miles across the country in a vintage camper, to falling in love with our new rescue kitten despite not being a cat guy. The list goes on and on. Give this man a medal.

> Don't strive to fit a square peg in a round hole. Find your fit. It's out there.

What I've learned over the past decade is how to meld my unconventional world with another human being. Our key strengths include: proclaiming love multiple times a day, distributing responsibilities {ex. he has litter box PM duty; I have AM duty}, believing our pug is the center of the universe and everything he does is pure perfection, being on the same page with many world views, having separate and mutual passions {ex. him, biking; me, yoga; us, travel}, openly sharing vulnerable feelings, making dates a priority {ex. we love documentaries, dining out, travel, events at the Kennedy Center, hosting dinner parties}, and being supportive during challenging times.

Is everything perfect? No. Perfection is bland. Oh, and unattainable. Just Friday we were having a discussion about eating habits. When he shared his view, I replied, "Well, your view is dumb." We laughed, and he noted how happy he was that we were able to be respectful despite differing opinions. Again, he's the adult. I use words like "dumb."

My best relationship advice? Don't strive to fit a square peg in a round hole. Find your fit. It's out there. And it may just be as close as across the street.

10. FREEDOM
February 2014

This piece was penned for my memoir writing class. The assignment was to find a photograph that's at least 10 years old, study it, slip back in time, and write an account of what I was doing, thinking, and feeling at that moment. Although the photo I reference is on a now-kaput computer, I recall the image vividly.

It was the summer of 2003 and I was on a two-week adventure to Mallorca and Ibiza, Spain, in celebration of my 30th birthday. Solo. After months of delay, I had just moved my 4-year-old yoga studio into a two-level space days before and there were many kinks to be ironed out. However, I knew 30 only came once and I was determined to make it special.

When asking around for insights on a memorable spot for this celebration *sans* families, I was consistently told Ibiza. Upon research, it felt like a pulsating spot for a single and curious 30-year-old to let loose.

Although my style of letting loose was kicked back topless on the beach reading an Ayn Rand biography or sitting solo for dinner on the beach reading *Good Business* by Mihaly Csikszentmihalyi. I wondered why the party promoters passed me by when circulating their fliers for the evening's must-attend DJ event.

One evening during a brief romance with a South African nearly 10 years my junior, I signed up for a sunset parasailing experience. The photo captures me up in the air with an orange parasail attached to my body and a pink-hued sunset on the horizon. It was snapped by a couple from Switzerland enjoying a romantic adventure on the island with an old school digital camera pre-smartphones.

The image shows me grinning from ear to ear, decked out in a Tranquil Space tee and capri leggings. I had thrown caution to the wind by escaping great responsibility to ensure a memorable transition from my 20s into a brand-new decade. Yet, there is also a sense of loneliness beneath the exterior. Back home was a questionable relationship that left me filled with emptiness and confusion, and a new business where I'd taken on great risk to expand, nurture, and grow. The risk was not only financial, but highly mental, physical, and emotional as well.

When I look at this image now, I am grateful for forgoing the responsible thing to stay in Washington, D.C. and oversee the fourth and fifth week of operation in our new home, teach classes, and build systems. Of course I remember this trip to Spain with much greater vividness than being home and working 15-hour days. There would be many more opportunities for those long days. I knew it. And lived it.

Purchasing that solo ticket to the islands in the spring of 2003 was a proud moment. It was me feeling a sense of control despite so many things feeling out of control at that time in my life—opening delays due to bureaucracy, an on-again off-again relationship, and the struggles of building a business solo without many support systems.

When I clicked purchase late one night after yet another harrowing day of teaching, giving, and feeling depleted, I knew I was doing the right thing. I felt it in my blood. I was eager for the sense of freedom that was to come. And on this particular night, it came in the form of parasailing solo by sunset.

How can you throw caution to the wind, experience a sense of freedom, and refill your well with a much-deserved adventure? The daily grind will be waiting for you when you return. Promise.

MY STORY NUGGETS

1. Creative dreams inspire motivation and growth.

2. Transitions and loss are overwhelmingly hard, yet part of the journey.

3. Life is an ongoing creation of memories, not to-dos.

~ MY STORY TAKEAWAYS ~

CHAPTER 3:
Yoga

Yoga is about making friends with life and with yourself. There is no lifestyle, no occupation, no situation that cannot be greatly enhanced by yoga. Yoga is not something that should be set apart from one's life. Rather it should become the taproot from which the other aspects of your life are nourished and regenerated.—Godfrey Devereaux

It was a frigid Wednesday morning in Summit County's snow-capped mountains. The kind where you can see your breath and need so many layers that you are practically left immobile. My wanderlust and backpacking buddy, Jina, pulled her 1995 teal Camaro into my apartment complex ten minutes later than expected. Always one to push my on-time comfort zone, I began to relax as we sang along to Alanis Morissette and made our way to the Silverthorne Recreation Center. The sun started to peek out from behind the jagged mountainside. The freshly fallen snow glistened. I had no idea that the trajectory of my life was about to change.

I was in my early 20s and reading about the mind and body benefits of yoga in *Cosmopolitan* and *Shape*. They proclaimed weight loss, relaxation, and flexibility. The local gym had added it to their class offerings, and I was hoping for a quick fix. Something to tone a body becoming fluffy from occasional binges {Everclear and Kool-Aid was the go-to} and quiet a whirling mind. Trying to make sense of life post-college, bruised from one too many failed relationships and an inability to find what I needed most, a sense of self.

Five of us placed our thick blue foam exercise mats sporadically across the floor with the Rockies as our backdrop. The teacher arrived and filled the room with a glowing presence. Middle-aged, wearing colorful baggy clothing with ponytail sitting atop her head, she possessed a sense of calm that was contagious. I settled into a cross-legged seated position on the floor and tried to make the most of the experience.

As the class progressed, we transitioned to downward-facing dog. I'd seen this pose peppered through-

> I had no idea that the trajectory of my life was about to change.

out women's magazines touting yoga as the end-all-be-all practice to tone the body and calm the mind and longed to look like the lean woman in that inverted V. Moving into a series called sun salutations, I began to feel my hips for the first time in the lunges. This dance-like sequence caused beads of perspiration to form on my forehead.

My mind slowed ever so slightly, and my body opened in a way that the skiing, snowboarding, and drinking of the past many months had not provided. There was a sense of coming home. Like the tranquility I'd found during the quiet moments of communion in my childhood church, but deeper and without religious sentiment.

In the closing backbends I felt pulsing in my heart center similar to that fluttery feeling when meeting a lover. When we came to rest on our backs for the final pose, *savasana*, I was smitten to have found exercise that included nap time.

This chapter highlights a smattering of yoga posts over the past decade—including office yoga poses, practicing headstand, favorite home yoga sequence, a restorative practice to recover from overindulgence, and more.

Tune into *Tranquility du Jour* podcasts #116, #194, #246 for more insights on yoga.

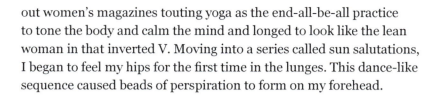

1. HAPPY HOLIDAYS
December 2004

The holidays are fast approaching. As I address numerous holiday cards and review to-do lists, I wonder where a little self-nurturing could be thrown into the mix. So, I wanted to share a few ideas to help stay in touch with your practice during the festivity hubbub.

1. **Stand on your head.** Literally. Headstand is a great way to get comfortable with your world upside down, learn to breathe through it, and come out feeling restored.

2. **Try tree pose.** While standing in long lines, shift your weight to one leg, place the opposite foot on your thigh, and breathe.

3. **Take a strong, proud *tadasana*.** A steady mountain pose helps to instill confidence. Picture yourself entering the holiday cocktail party where you know no one with grace, dignity, a scooped tailbone and a strong mountain-like purpose. You deserve to be there and for people to know your fabulous self.

4. **Breathe fully.** Nothing like a full, deep yogic breath to bring you back to the body and remove you from list-making in your head. Notice your breath in hectic holiday situations and restore your sanity.

5. **Let go**. Aunt Helga's annual, "so when ARE you getting married/getting a real job," is sure to annoy. But it is how you react that intensifies the internal struggle. Answer with stern dignity, "As I've mentioned before, I love being single/serving in the Peace Corps and am thoroughly enjoying the life I'm leading." Letting go of the desire to control another person {especially family} will free up an amazing amount of energy.

6. **Carve out "me time."** Journal write, take a hot bath, light candles, buy yourself a holiday treat, sip herbal tea, paint.

7. **Host a soirée**. Invite over your closest friends for some yoga, annual reflection, new year intention setting, and overall connection.

8. **Get creative**. Give gifts that benefit your relationship. Two tickets to the opera, a coupon for a day at the museum and dinner on you, a homemade dinner on the date of their choice, two registrations to a yoga workshop . . . all of these ideas allow you to spend time with your beloved AND benefit from the experience.

I hope these help you carve out some precious practice time over the holidays. Live luxuriously by paying special attention to your body and looking for ways to throw yoga into the mix, both on and off the mat.

Anthology Extras: Being a Beginner
January 2014

There is something invigorating, most humbling, and slightly humiliating about being a beginner. As a practicing yogini for nearly two decades and as teacher for 15 years, I have come to feel fairly confident on the mat. Sure I've weathered many setbacks ranging from injury to surgeries to declined energy and aging, but nothing is quite like the challenge of being a beginner.

Tuesday morning, I scuttled across the floor like a crab in my beginning ballet class. It was my first return to dance since dabbling in ballet, hip-hop, and other classes over the past decade {and always feeling like the odd woman out}. Over the past few weeks I've been taking barre classes at my gym and, again, struggling to keep up. It reminds me of my days of step aerobics where I couldn't grasp the choreography and flailed around like a menace. Anyone else recall the horror of step aerobics?

On Monday night I asked my barre teacher if it would get easier. What I really meant was, "Will I always be the worst in the room?" but I couldn't bring myself to ask *that* question. She assured me that it wasn't meant to ever be easy and that this was good for me to be learning to move my body in a new way, mentioning "having been at the top of my game for years."

Um, top of my game is a grand overstatement, but I know what she meant about being used to and comfortable with a certain style of movement.

Alas, I will continue to put myself out there and expand my body and mind's horizons {despite feeling like a crab}. I know it's good for me. I recognize that it pushes my comfort zone. And I know it enhances my compassion for beginners who cross my path as a teacher.

Hip hip hooray for new experiences on the barre, on the mat, in the kitchen, and in life. Where can you be a beginner this year? Try it! I think you'll like it.

2. OFFICE YOGA
January 2005

Weaving yoga into your daily routine, even if you can't make your favorite studio class, contributes to a tranquil state of being. Taking time at the office or while out and about to connect within is crucial to a healthy mindset. Incorporate this yoga sequence into your daily life for a 15-minute "mental health break."

Begin by sitting on the edge of your seat with feet hip width apart and flat on the ground. Extend the crown of the head toward the ceiling, creating an elongated spine and connect to your breath. The yoga poses below begin from this basic starting position.

1. **Neck and shoulder rolls**: Inhale deeply. Exhale and allow the eyes to close. Inhale, lengthen the spine and slowly lower the right ear to the right shoulder. Exhale, lower the chin to the chest. Inhale, lift the left ear to the left shoulder. Exhale, lower the chin to the chest. Repeat five times.

Inhale, roll the shoulders forward and up to your ears. Exhale, rolling the shoulders back and towards the floor, allow the shoulder blades to slide down the back. Repeat five times in both directions.

Benefits: rests the eyes to help prevent eye strain; lubricates and stretches the neck joints; relieves tension in the neck, shoulders, and upper back.

2. **Seated cat and cow**: Clasp the seat of the chair, palms down and fingers pointing towards the floor. Inhale, bring the chest forward and draw the shoulder blades together, take a slight back bend in cow position. Exhale, bring the belly towards the back of the chair, allow the shoulders to fall forward into cat position. Repeat five times, concentrating on coordinating each movement with an inhale and an exhale.

Benefits: warms and elongates the spine, relieves back tension, opens the heart center.

3. **Chair twists**: Inhale, lengthen the head towards the ceiling. Exhale, bring the left hand to the outside of your right leg, and twist to the right side. Place the right hand on the seat back. Allow the head to follow the twist of the spine and the eyes to gaze beyond the chair back. Inhale, come back to center and repeat on the other side. Repeat a few times, moving with the breath.

Benefits: whittles the waist; stretches the spine, shoulders and hips; relieves lower back, neck, and sciatica pain; aids in digestion; massages internal organs which pushes out toxins and allows the organs to refill with fresh blood.

4. **Eagle arms**: Inhale, stretch the arms out to the sides. Exhale, bring your left arm under your right arm. Cross both arms at the elbows, point the elbows to the floor and fingers up toward the ceiling. Place the palms of the hands together. Inhale, raise your elbows toward shoulder height and move the hands away from your face. Exhale, slowly draw circles with the elbows in one direction and then the other. Repeat on the other side.

Benefits: firms upper arms and stretches the upper back/shoulder muscles.

5. **Seated child's pose**: Inhale, lengthen the spine toward the ceiling, exhale fold forward placing the chest on the thighs. Allow the arms to drop to the floor. Breathe deeply and relax for 30 seconds. Inhale, engage the abs and raise the upper body to a sitting position.

Variations: {1} turtle pose: while in child's pose, open the legs to hip distance. Thread arms between the legs and around the calves. Grasp the outside of the foot with the hand. {2} Hands clasped behind the back pose: while in child's pose, reach the arms behind the back and clasp the fingers together. Lower the hands toward the head.

Benefits: rejuvenates the body; stretches the spine; massages the abdominal area.

6. **Ankle and wrist rolls**: Roll ankles and wrists in clockwise circles. Repeat counter-clockwise.

Benefits: lubricates ankle and wrist joints; promotes blood circulation, eases carpal tunnel syndrome.

7. **Walking meditation**: As you walk to the copier or water cooler, bring awareness to each step and movement. Notice sensations in your body, concentrate on your breath and practice awareness of your surroundings. Feel a sense of tranquility throughout your body. As Thich Nhat Hanh says, "Walk as if your feet are kissing the earth."

Benefits: brings mindfulness into the mundane, creates tranquility.

May these small changes to your daily routine bring relief from the many directions in which you are pulled.

3. YOGA CONFERENCE TAKEAWAYS
May 2005

Greetings from the land of cheese. Midwesterners are loving the TranquiliT manifesto tees and we totally sold out on the first day. I LOVE the people here. Amazing what not living in the hustle of a city does for folks' demeanor.

The drive from the Milwaukee airport to the resort center where the conference is held was a gentle reminder of my roots. Sooo very Oklahomaish! Plains, not so many trees, nice "salt of the earth" people happy to assist you, hills, farm houses, roadside stands, and barns. Considering I haven't been home in three years, this part of the country feels nice.

After a full day of TranquiliT selling, I enjoyed Rodney Yee's keynote on serving, followed by a Kirtan with Dave Stringer. *Govinda, Gopala, Gopala, Govinda* . . .

Serving. Do we ever really think of what that means? As a yoga teacher, I was taught to think of every class I teach as being of service. Yee's talk was a great reminder of this. Can't we be of service with EVERY role we hold—teacher, student, mother, daughter, partner, consultant, assistant? How would life be different if we approached each day with "how can I serve {or make a difference} today?" WOW!

And, he went on to talk about how Americans overwork {really?} and that realizing the power of *savasana* can be our way of being of service. I liken this to putting on your own mask before your child's on an airplane. We have to replenish ourselves before we can help others.

He also requested that we evaluate our life, cut back on something that isn't serving us anymore {relationship, job, situation, etc.}, use the new found time to restore, and then replace it with being of service. I loved the concept. I will continue to ponder what that could be for me. I can never think of anything to remove, only things I want to add. Hmmm, may be why I'm a little tired.

Anyway, he and Dave Stringer commented on the power of yoga and how important it is to "relish triangle, relish *utkatasana*." How often do you find yourself saying, "When is she going to let us out of this pose? When is *savasana*?" They both reiterated how, in life, we deal with the same thing. We're in an uncomfortable or challenging pose/situation, and we keep looking for an escape rather than softening into it. I get what they're saying, but when your pet is sick, your partner is unbearable, and you don't know how bills will get paid, it can be hard to "soften" or "let go." What I take away from it is that in THESE times, we are learning valuable lessons, we are gaining strength and wisdom, and that there is no reason to rush the process. It has a timetable beyond our control.

One final takeaway from Dave's chats in between chants was the notion of "on and off the mat," one of my fave phrases, and how life isn't really separated into the two parts. Our on and off are one and the same. I'll ponder that one, but I really liked his blending of life and yoga as a whole.

Overall, Wisconsin has been fabulous, and I've met some great people. I believe in synchronicity and it seems to play out at every tradeshow I do. I meet and am connected with such like-hearted people. The world is full of them, we know that, but it is always fun to be reminded of it in synchronistic ways.

4. YOGA AS A LIFESTYLE
May 2005

Tranquil Space is a lifestyle-focused yoga studio that serves to enhance lives on and off the yoga mat. But what does this really mean? Having reflected on this a lot recently, I wanted to share the evolutionary process. In my first teacher training six years ago, I consciously decided that I didn't want to become a yoga teacher who leads students through a series of poses and then simply sends them on their way. So when I began teaching in my living room, I knew I wanted to offer them more—ways to live life more fully, ways to explore their creative side, ways to connect with other like-minded Washingtonians, and ways to find their edge. The edge is that space beyond the comfort zone, well before pain.

Living yoga principles off the mat becomes a way of life that reflects values and attitudes. By viewing yoga in this way, I explored how to teach yoga off the mat to allow students to find their own path and personalize it. Practicing yoga may simply be moving through the poses when you first come across a yoga mat, but the practice also lovingly teaches connection to the more subtle aspects of yourself.

For example, yoga has helped me become a much stronger person, both physically and emotionally. Yes, *chaturanga* seemed like an impossible feat at the beginning, now I can't imagine life without it. Yes, having to initiate an uncomfortable conversation has never been easy, but somehow yoga has helped empower me to do so. Also, by paying attention to my truth {*satya*}, I recognize the alternative—I'm uneasy about something but not being authentic by ignoring it.

Yoga is not about perfection, judgment, regret, following blindly, or a belief that there is only one way. Yoga is personalized for every practitioner and that is the beauty of the practice. Yoga as a lifestyle is about authenticity, making value-based decisions, empowerment, self-study {*svadhyaya*}, compassion, presenting your best self to the world, passion, intention, moderation {*brahmacharya*}, and self-nurturing.

Tranquil Space is a special haven where I hope others will be inspired to live life in a way that shines. After all, that is why you are here, to shine as brightly as possible! You were drawn to the practice for a reason, and I encourage you to explore this deeply. The mission of Tranquil Space is taking principles of yoga out of the studio and into daily life. I believe this to be so important that Tranquil Space offers workshops that help you explore your practice in areas such as mindful money management, conscious cooking, and even knitting. Some share that they live their yoga through self-care practices such as pedicures and massages.

Continue your exploration of yoga as a lifestyle and enjoy the constant evolution of it. Relish in the notion that you are challenging yourself in subtle and overt ways every time you step onto the mat. Honor the intentions and dedications that you create. Begin each day with the

What lies before us and what lies behind us is nothing compared to what lies within us.
—Ralph Waldo Emerson

one-pointed focus we seek in yoga, and end each day in gratitude. Unleash your unlimited potential within. Let your yoga practice be as unique as you are. Embrace the teachings, hold onto what resonates with you, and continue to live your life one pose at a time.

5. TURNING YOUR WORLD UPSIDE DOWN
July 2005

Inversions are a funny animal when you first join a yoga class. You want me to do what?? As we progress in our practice, it's fun to see how some bodies actually begin to crave turning upside down. I equate it to a similar sensation I feel in my hamstrings after two days off of practice—they actually ache for opening. I've had students tell me that they love closing their office door and going up into headstand mid-day. For those of you a bit timid about turning your world upside down, read on for headstand tips and stages:

Make sure you are strong in downward-facing dog, *chaturanga*, and up dog before progressing into a full headstand. If you're still struggling with vinyasa, don't worry, I'll offer some modifications to help build strength.

Begin in downward facing dog on your yoga mat in comfy, fitted clothes. Turning upside down with your shirt coming over your head prevents the *dristi* {focus point}.

Come onto your forearms with the elbows directly under your shoulders and interlace your hands. Press your forearms into the mat and keep the shoulders lifted without sinking shoulders to ears.

If you feel strong here, place the top of your head in between your clasped hands. Shift the weight distribution off of your head, into your forearms so that you have lots of space along the neck.

Next, walk your feet toward your hands until they won't go anymore without your legs bending. Again, stay here if this is enough challenge. Getting comfortable upside down is no easy feat.

Engage the core, bend the knees and bring your knees above your hips. Stay here. Most people try to kick up at the wall, banging into the wall without connecting to the core. Surrender desire for the final product and enjoy being where you are.

If you're steady, straighten the legs and extend towards the heavens. Think *tadasana* {mountain pose} turned upside down.

Voilà, you're inverting and replenishing your internal organs!

Disclaimer: Please consult your doctor if you have any health conditions that would prevent you from turning upside down such as glaucoma or endometriosis {during menstruation}. Also, if you don't feel steady, return to the previous stage or release slowly down to child's pose.

Turning upside down offers respite from our normal upright existence. Enjoy the sensations, savor the stages, don't rush the process, and honor your continued progression both on and off the mat.

6. FAVE HOME YOGA SEQUENCE
December 2005

I'm a hip girl, LOVE hip-opening poses. Anytime a teacher asks for a request, I wave my little hand begging for anything hip related. My home practice is no exception. I'm sharing my fave home sequence to inspire you to bring life into your hips, and take a little you time during the harried holidays.

1. **Connect to your breath.**

2. **Begin with sun salutations** to awaken your spirit and get your yoga juices flowing.

3. **Take a few standing poses:** warrior 1, warrior 2, reverse warrior, side angle, revolved side angle, triangle, revolved triangle, pyramid, etc.

4. **Take your fave balancing pose:** dancer, tree {perfect for the season}, warrior 3, big toe stretch, eagle, etc.

5. **Hips, hips and more hips:** pigeon, dove, cow face, double pigeon, lotus, *baddha konasana*, half splits, full splits, lunge with back knee dropped, et cetera. Ahhhh, these are the BEST, especially this time of the year.

6. **Try a backbend or two:** bridge, camel, wheel, etc.

7. **Inversion:** shoulderstand, legs up the wall, forearm stand, handstand.

8. ***Savasana*:** your reward, soak up the benefits of your practice for five to 15 minutes.

~ Reader Feedback ~

Kimberly Wilson's blog has always been a great source of information, ideas, and inspiration for me. She has a clear-cut idea of the way her world and life works, and has the courage to tell her readers about it through her blog, books, and podcasts. Kimberly's positive outlook and the search for something more is contagious. I always look forward to her Week in Review and Weekend Wish List. It's inspiring to see one woman take on all that and more, yet still leave time for what is important.

I am thankful for her blog and all the great words of wisdom and experience of being an entrepreneur that she passed on to me as a reader for the past decade. Kimberly has an interesting way of drawing people in and teaching them how and why through her cool eyes. She talks about having professional crushes and I hope she realizes how many fellow entrepreneurs, yogis, and do-gooders add Kimberly to their own professional crush list!

Darlynn Tacinelli, Florida
thelittleblogdress.com

7. YOGINI GONE WILD
April 2006

After spending most of the day hibernating in bed due to one too many cosmos, I have been moving slowly this evening. Those neurons just aren't firing so quickly. Le Beau says it's good to have some down time. Instead, I feel antsy that I didn't get enough done. It IS supposed to be my day off, but I didn't even step outside to see the beautiful weather. Ahhh, tomorrow's a new day filled with sunshine, productivity, and a clear head.

I wanted to share a fave restorative sequence to help you get through your not-so-fabulous/one-too-many-cosmos days. Have a blanket or bolster nearby for #2-5.

Note: Extra doses of tranquility include a lavender-filled eyepillow, a scented candle burning nearby, the phone turned off, rosebud salve on your lips, and a yummy essential oil rubbed onto your temples.

1. **Legs up the wall.** Begin on your back and extend your legs up a wall. Place your bum as close to the wall as possible. For a shoulder opener, bring the arms up over your head to reach for opposite elbows. Notice your breath and feel the body soften. For a variation, open your legs to a wide V. Or, bend your knees and place the soles of the feet together. Stay here as long as feels good.

2. Slowly roll over to your right side, rest a few breaths, and press up to a seated position. Take a blanket or bolster and roll it tightly lengthwise. Place the blanket vertically behind your tailbone, and lie back over the blanket. Let your arms splay out to the sides or up over your head.

3. Roll to your right side and sit up, place the blanket horizontally under the shoulder blades {at your bra line} and roll back over the blanket. This one is a huge heart opener and so juicy.

4. Roll to your right side and slowly lift up to a child's pose. Bring your big toes together and open your knees wide. Place the blanket between the knees and rest over the blanket{s}, turn your head to either side.

5. Place a rolled blanket horizontally under your shoulder blades and one under your knees. Let those arms splay out behind the blanket. Yummy mountain brook pose. Ahhhhhh.

Anthology Extras: Marking
January 2014

While doing three-hour yoga classes in New York City at the start of the New Year, I noticed that I had been marking my way through many poses. Marking is a dance term. It is beneficial for saving energy for the big performance, but not necessarily in yoga.

In yoga, the way we live our life is the performance.

After learning to modify based on my two surgeries in 2010 {thumb and shoulder} and adjusting for age and energy since then, there has been a big shift into a more relaxed mode. Relaxed is not bad, but going through the motions and not doing poses full out {another dance term} isn't ideal.

As I confessed this to another yogini who's been on the mat for also nearly two decades, I began to ponder how this has affected my practice recently. Being in a ballroom full of intense New York City yogis giving the practice their all was the perfect kick in the pants I needed.

And I began to wonder where in life I may also be marking. It's a big philosophical question that stems from my simple observation of not giving my practice my all.

Take a moment to notice where you, too, may be marking in life. Your morning routine. Time with loved ones. Exercise. Writing. Creativity.

It happens. And it's good to note without judgment in order to begin to steer yourself back to living full out. That's where it gets juicy.

8. JIVAMUKTI GRADUATION
May 2007

> What a ride! I've learned so much. I've been exhausted. I've challenged myself. My neck has ached. I've set off fire alarms burning incense.

Wow! I got through last night's final exam, woke up for the last time at 7:10 a.m. to Krishna Das as my alarm, and had my finale Jivamukti practice with the 110 others at this month-long teacher training. I get a bit sentimental about the ending of anything. However, I'm also terribly excited to share what I've learned, to figure out how to incorporate it, to return to reality outside this microcosm, to hug my pug and kitties, to sleep in my spacious double bed, to wake up with Le Beau, to explore these dietary changes in my real life, and to savor the many subtle shifts that have transpired this month.

I'm also delighted to share that I've had successful neti pot experiences the past few days. Yay! I figured out the right tilt of the head. Many peeps' allergies are flaring up with all the blooming trees here and using the neti pot helps to alleviate them. Try it out. Maybe they even make them in pink or leopard-print.

Also, there is a must-have book that I encourage you to get if you're interested in learning more about the Yoga Sutras. It is *The Essential Yoga Sutra: Ancient Wisdom for Your Yoga* by Geshe Michael Roach {who also wrote *The Diamond Cutter*, which I have recommended before}. He's brilliant AND it outlines the four chapters of the Yoga Sutras in easy-to-grasp commentary.

Last night my new Canadian pal Jennifer came into my room for neti pot salt and saw the stargazer lilies Le Beau had brought to me. She mentioned that they were too fragrant for her. Then I pointed out my lavender plug-in, lit a few candles, sprayed pillow spray on my linens, and put lavender pulse point creme on her temples. Now THAT is fragrance, honey!

Thank you for joining me on this incredible journey. What a ride! I've learned so much. I've been exhausted. I've challenged myself. My neck has ached. I've set off fire alarms burning incense. I've cried at upsetting films. I've struggled with my neti pot. I've tried to stay connected with "reality" back home and struggled with the shifts between here and there. I've observed interesting patterns in myself on the mat {I struggle with backbends} and off the mat {I'm reactionary and have trouble letting go}.

Sweet Le Beau is en route to join me for graduation tonight, and I'm excited for the beautiful drive home tomorrow—and the fun stops along the way {Tarjay, grocery store, lookout spots}. *Namaste.*

9. COMMUNICATION
May 2008

I took a class with the lovely Max Strom today on refining communication as a yoga teacher. I find the whole concept of communication FASCINATING! There is a whole center for Nonviolent Communication and I'm dying to learn more.

Max's tips were:

Make eye contact, smile when you walk into the room

Be vulnerable, share personal stories, remind students that if you can do it, so can they

Record your class and try your class at home later. Observe patterns

Teach to multiple levels by offering modifications and variations

Start with the basic version first {ex. forearm to thigh in side angle}

Teach by repetition, it's the best way to learn new things

Find your authentic voice—avoid *innnnnn-haallllllleeeee, exxxxhhhhhhaaallllle*

In some way, these tips can apply in our every day communication off the mat. It's always best to make eye contact, acknowledge people, and be fully present when in communication. Ever been with a friend who checks their email while you're in conversation? I've been on the giving and the receiving end of that, and it doesn't feel good. By observing how we communicate—the numerous "ums," the stammering, the avoiding of a real issue—we can grow in improving our communication skills.

And, of course, finding our authentic voice, style, and *modus operandi* ensures we're true to ourselves, which will attract those who resonate with us. One thing I learned early on in my teaching—while transitioning from a slow style based in Integrative Yoga Therapy to a more rigorous style based on Ashtanga—is that I cannot be the teacher for everyone. Some people love our evolution as teachers or beings, but others will not. Embrace those who do and know that the others will resonate with someone else. THAT was a very liberating lesson early on.

In the interim, explore your communication—written, verbal, body language, eye contact—and note ways to grow. Communication is an ongoing journey.

10. YOGA DEFINED
September 2009

Bon National Yoga Month. Yoga translates to "union," and it offers a way to live life with mindful flair. The physical poses and breath work associated with yoga in the West are catalysts, but not the full picture of this ancient practice. Yoga is a way of being. My favorite mantra *Lokah Samastah Sukhino Bhavantu* translates to "May all beings everywhere be happy and free." *That* is yoga!

You're often in motion—browsing a bookstore, sipping tea at a café, volunteering at a local shelter—and you can find balance by staying connected to your practice off the yoga mat. For example, instead of growing impatient while waiting for a late subway train, shift your weight onto your right leg, and place your left foot on your right ankle to practice the tranquility-invoking tree pose. Or practice taking long, full breaths. You can find peace within the pandemonium by spontaneously practicing the thoughtful principles of yoga in your everyday.

Yoga can transform life on so many levels. A few benefits include: increased confidence; attention to the impact of situations, people, and food on your body; the chance to slow down and take a break from life on the mat; meeting a community of like-hearted people; breathing deeply to ground yourself in sticky situations; improved sleep patterns; a connection to your inner voice; toned body; relief from pain, headaches, and stress. Oh, and the list goes on and on, and it varies among yogis. Needless to say, yoga can have a profound effect on your *joie de vivre*!

May this moment provide the push you need to deepen your yoga practice. Whether it is the practice of poses, deep breaths, or embracing the mantra presented above, you ARE a yogini. Let yoga ooze from your spirit as easily as you draft a memo, nurture your family, walk your dog, or do anything that comes second nature. Yoga is about living in a way that contributes to others, and if you achieve headstand along the way, so be it. Bask in being you—mindfully and authentically you. *Namaste*.

YOGA NUGGETS

1. A little bit of yoga does a body real good.

2. Embrace being a beginner and notice where you're marking in life.

3. Yoga is a lifestyle, not just what one does on the mat.

~ YOGA TAKEAWAYS ~

CHAPTER 4: Lifestyle

The purpose of life is to live it, to taste experience to the utmost, to reach out eagerly and without fear for newer and richer experience. —Eleanor Roosevelt

Books line the walls and are tucked into various nooks and crannies. Chandeliers hang from the ceiling and adorn the room with just the right amount of light. A candle and stick of incense is always lit. White covers garnish white furniture to protect it from black pets, twinkle lights hang by the fireplace, and large sliding glass doors create a cozy setting within 600 square feet. The Pink Palace offers a respite from daily life and nurtures all my senses.

Over the years I've sought to carve out a lifestyle that represents who I am and what I desire. For example, since the passing of my Gramma and going on semi-sabbatical, I've been relishing a newfound sense of spaciousness—something I craved for years. Loss and grief have a way of putting things in perspective and, sometimes, completely shifting one's lifestyle.

Lifestyle extends well beyond our home environment and into our habits, attitudes, and tastes that make up the way we live. Many posts in *Tranquility du Jour* speak to an ongoing journey to infuse my lifestyle with tranquility. Inside you'll find tips for blissful slumbering, my definition of tranquility, lessons from France, the value of unplugging, and more.

Tune into Tranquility du Jour podcasts #181, #259, #310 for more insights on lifestyle.

1. HOW TO BE SICK
February 2009

Down for the count with some yucky bug. Started yesterday with what I thought was low energy, intensified to full on "bugginess." While lounging in bed, I wanted to pull together tips to assist with an uninvited bug.

1. **Soak in the tub**. Fresh out of my third soak in less than 24 hours. Helps relieve achiness.

2. **Sip oodles of tea**. Downing Throat Coat tea like it's going out of style. Even double bagging it.

3. **Infuse your water with emergenC**. It makes your water taste like Tang {yum!} and is full of vitamin C.

4. **Release guilt.** Yes, deadlines are looming. Yes, there are many other things you *should* be doing. Yes, lying around doesn't feel terribly productive. But your body needs to heal.

5. **Curl up with your beloved furry friend.** Le Pug is providing cuddly company and it can be nice bonding time.

6. **Keep technology nearby.** ONLY if you *must* be accessible, have your laptop, planner, and cell phone within reach to handle any emergencies or promises you made pre-bug.

7. **Stay grateful.** It can be easy to take energy and health for granted.

8. **Let go**. Bugs find their way to you. Fighting it saps energy. Release into it, savor the down time, and let go of trying to control.

9. **Read.** Keep a good book nearby to pick up, savor a few words, and surrender to when energy lessens.

I hope these few tips help you stay sane while waiting for the unwelcomed bug to move along. Here's to your health!

Anthology Extras: Slumbering Bliss
September 2009

Considering my lifestyle, I'm very serious about sleep. At least eight hours {preferably nine} is a must. If it looks like it may not happen due to my bad habit of staying up way past my bedtime to handle that elusive one more thing, I begin to panic and proclaim, "I must fall asleep within 2.5 minutes to get my full eight hours." Then I quickly don my eyepillow, insert earplugs, strategically place piles of pillows, ensure a cup of water is nearby, and curl up for slumbering bliss.

In *Hip Tranquil Chick* I outline my savvy sleeping tips:

1. **Invest in earplugs**—great for travel
2. **Indulge in an eyepillow**—try one with an elastic band to stay in place while tossing and turning
3. **Put on a soothing CD**—*j'adore* sounds of rain and waterfalls
4. **Drink of plenty of water**—stay hydrated
5. **Spray the pillow**—lavender is helpful
6. **Apply lip balm**—keep your face and lips moisturized {I love almond oil}

Tranquility Tip: have pen and paper nearby to capture middle-of-the-night ideas and random to-dos that come to mind. This will get them out of your head and onto paper so you can slumber with a clear mind.

May your sleep be filled with tranquility.

~ Reader Feedback ~

Tranquility du Jour has been a welcome email that comes to give me pause, to sit back and see where Kimberly has been, who she has seen, what she has accomplished, and when she gets time to reflect, I love what she writes. When she becomes reflective, I am there with her and realizing what I want/need to change. Often, she seems to be speaking only to me.

I must say that I enjoy seeing what Kimberly has accomplished in just one week with her Week in Review. Sometimes one of the items she lists, I think to myself, that I could have done that if I would just allow me to open a time for ME!

The Mindful Monday posts make me think of new and exciting venues to try during the week. Her announcements for her podcasts with an introduction of her featured guest reminds me to get it downloaded so I can meet someone new. Wednesday Well-Being leads me to a new path of openness. Things I Love is one of my favorites because I often will travel to the site she supplies and have many copies of crafts and recipes that she had found online. I am fond of the craft ideas because she always gets the link so I can look at directions.

When reading about her activism with animals, she introduced me to books on the subject and I am struggling to go without meat due to the reading and have taken the pledge to go on Meatless Mondays. If reading her blog only does that, she has saved lives!

I love seeing her new clothing line when introduced on her blog, along how to pack. It includes several signature pieces from her TranquiliT line that travel beautifully.

Since I am Kimberly's mother, you might say that I have to say these things because I am partial when it comes to her. I promise that could not be more true, but if you have read this far and been a fan of her blog, you also know that *Tranquility du Jour* is a very special way to spend time learning to be a better you. I truly wonder who does not want to feel better at the end of the day about yourself and your world.

Linda Ann Ewing Wilson, Oklahoma

2. TIPS O' TRANQUILITY
July 2010

As I continue to procrastinate on my 15-page paper due tomorrow {grrr}, I figured I should do a blog post, too. And maybe clean, organize, plan next year . . .

Saturday I gave a talk to a lovely group of ladies who were in town for an all-day workshop. Donning a fall one-shoulder TranquiliT sample and a knit pink cap, I shared snippets from my 11-year entrepreneurial journey along with fave tips for tranquility in work and play.

A few highlights include:

1. **Spirituality is a priority**. Connect within through ongoing reflection, learning, and growing. Write in your journal. Connect with your breath.

2. **Take action**. Take a moment to note where your time and energy are focused. Reflect on where you want your time and energy to go. Explore ways to shift if reality doesn't match your dreams.

3. **Your life is art.** Color outside the lines. Indulge in an artist date. Browse a bookstore or art gallery. Get crafty. Snap inspiration throughout your day with a digital camera or smartphone.

4. **Exude style**. Don clothing that exudes your personality. Send thank you notes. Communicate clearly. Exercise. Nourish your palate.

5. **Leave a legacy.** Launch something to make a difference. Share your expertise. Tweet your message. Diversify. Give back to the community. Make a difference.

What are *your* favorite ways to find tranquility in work and play?

3. CRAFTING A SCHEDULE
August 2011

In an effort to carve out a more balanced schedule with room to breathe, space between appointments, ample time for my varied passions, and a tranquil flow, I crafted a new schedule for September—December. Although it is only day three, it's working well thus far and feeling so much more spacious. Time will tell. I already see a couple of needed tweaks, but I'm feeling good about the fresh canvas. I'll create an updated schedule once I try this one out over the next few weeks. The new one will be a full-fledged artist date with ephemera, glitter glue, and all!

Here are a few tips for creating your own schedule:

1. **Print spreadsheet** from my168hours.com.

2. **Gather markers,** your planner, and open space.

3. **Pen in your non-negotiables** such as sleep, office hours, classes, weekly appointments.

4. **Fill in your ideal** bedtime, movement {yoga, gym, dance, etc.}, and social schedule.

5. **Review to ensure it feels fluid.** If not, see if there are changes you can make or puzzle pieces you can move around. Does it feel balanced? Is it all work and no play or all play and no work?

Bonus: Are your daily activities moving you in the direction of your dreams? If not, it's time for a change.

Ooh la la, an opportunity to start anew, revamp, and prepare for tackling your dreams one by one.

> Are your daily activities moving you in the direction of your dreams? If not, it's time for a change.

4. SETTLING IN
June 2012

The past two weeks in France have been filled with new connections, heaps of hosting, seeking new experiences, and settling in to a different pace of life. Surprisingly exhausting, yet incredibly rewarding. Leaving the comfort of home and setting out with Le Beau, Le Pug, and luggage in tow makes for an adventure.

From getting proficient with *parlez-vous anglais?* to freezing when someone says *bonjour mademoiselle* by randomly responding *pardon* and running off, and accidentally ordering a *café of water* instead of a *carafe of water*—it's been one embarrassing giggle after another. I mean, after all, you have to be able to laugh at yourself, right?

There are a few beautiful things that have emerged from my journey and I'm hopeful that they will become part of my repertoire and inspire you, too.

1. **Take time to sip tea**. Sitting at a *café* to truly savor a pot of tea is beautiful. It's a true gift to curl up with a pot of tea, good book, and pug on your lap. Why rush the process with a to-go cup?

2. **There is no hurry**. There is not the rush, rush mentality I live by back home. There seems to be a true appreciation for smelling the roses.

3. **Exude style**. A scarf and a striped shirt seem to be a part of everyone's wardrobe. There are lots of colorful pants and blazers on men and a true sense of presenting oneself beautifully to the world.

4. **Beauty is everywhere.** Lordie, I've seen ads in the metro set within a gorgeous ornate gold frame. Also, *fleur* shops are everywhere and I picked up beautiful peonies for our hotel room this week. Appreciation for simple touches {doilies with tea, artistic garden tickets, ornate train stations} seems to be an art form here.

5. **Always say hello**. When greeting a service provider or entering a store, there is the standard *bonjour* before launching into one's request. I like that sense of formality and decorum.

We have four weeks left on this journey and I'm grateful for each moment. My hope is slowing down, serving fully, and filling with fresh ideas. I'm brewing up lots of new offerings for *Tranquility du Jour*.

5. SIGNATURE STYLE
December 2012

Everyday style. The joy of flair. A sprinkle of comfort. Dollops of sparkle. Since my early days of hiking the hills of Oklahoma toting a purse, I've been a fan of dressing as an art form.

A social work classmate recently described my style as "Anthropologie Goth" while another pulled me aside after our final class to ask if something had happened to me since I always don noir. Hmmm, I'll take "Anthropologie Goth," *merci*!

As you'll see from the smattering of style pics on the blog, daily dress up continues to be a favorite part of my day and offers the continued opportunity for creative expression. This past year I played with pairing stripes and patterns, shorts with blazers and tights, and fancy, fluffy skirts with t-shirts.

Working in a corporate environment of closed-toe shoes over the past few months of my social work internship has added a new way to play with self-expression within defined "normalcy." As you can imagine, quite different from a yoga studio. Adding colored tights and a reclaimed blazer over my TranquiliT layers is my go-to for weathering this creative challenge.

In a recent podcast interview with Courtney Carver {Tune into *Tranquility du Jour* podcast #259}, we discussed her Project 333 where you dress with 33 items for 3 months. *J'adore* this idea as many relate to having a closet full of clothes and nothing to wear. Paring down to what we do wear and releasing the rest is genius. After living out of two bags for six weeks of travel recently, I came home to find way more stuff than I needed and have been on a minimizing kick ever since. I've kept myself out of tempting stores such as Target {where I rarely left without a new pair of vegan flats}, donated heaps of clothing I wasn't wearing regularly, and begun to narrow down to basics.

As we move into this New Year, explore daily dress up as a work of art that fits your daily life. In the newly released *Tranquility du Jour Daybook*, I describe this as "Let your daily dress reflect your personality, lifestyle, and signature style. Always add a dose of flair and don't forget your smile, good attitude, and vintage accessory."

Here's to a daily routine that offers you the exuberant joy you had as a little girl playing dress up. As the Queen {Madonna} says, "Express yourself, don't repress yourself."

6. WHAT YOU CONSUME
February 2013

While sharing my understanding of practicing the *yamas* and *niyamas* at Friday's "living your yoga" 21-day challenge finale, we discussed *saucha*. *Saucha* is a *niyama* {lifestyle observance} translated as clarity, purity, or cleanliness and relates to our thoughts, words, and actions. As you may know, the juicy *yamas* and *niyamas* are the first two limbs of the eight-limb yoga path—strategically placed before *asana* {the physical poses we practice on our colorful non-slip mats}.

When discussing the many modern-day ways we can practice these 10 foundational principles, I love exploring how applicable they are to our daily decision-making. Including what to eat, how to communicate, and how to spend time. Yes, big and profound to tiny and mundane decisions.

Saucha has always been a favorite of mine for reflection and as we move into the spring season, it felt like a good one to focus on here. Spring encourages cleaning out closets, detoxing, shedding the weight {literally and figuratively} of winter. Why not let *saucha* be your guide?

Notice how you feel when your body is filled with greens and whole grains versus pizza and ice cream. Observe the difference when your desk is tidy with neatly stacked folders versus papers and tea cups strewn about. Pay attention to your heart rate and sensations in your chest center when your mind feels focused as opposed to monkey-like.

According to author and psychotherapist Stephen Cope, "For me, *saucha* means both physical and mental hygiene. You want to keep your thoughts uncluttered so you can feel free from afflictive emotions; you keep your body and environment in order, to create a sense of calm."

> Always aim at complete harmony of thought and word and deed. Always aim at purifying your thoughts and everything will be well.
> —Gandhi

How can you find a sense of tranquility in your physical and mental space? Can you: Replace soda with water? Shift hours of mindless TV watching or Facebook updating with mindful reading? Change moments of doing into a sprinkling of being? Reframe quick, terse email replies with thoughtful, kind ones?

Explore your daily habits over this next month and notice what small, *sauchic* shifts you can make to create a lifestyle that aligns with your values. Your body and mind, as well as your family and friends, will be grateful. May this new month and fresh season offer you moments of mindful tranquility.

7. SNAIL MAIL
May 2013

Bonjour from rainy Paris. After a lovely dinner with a retreater, studio boutique manager, and TranquiliT-lover who just happened to be on my same flight over, I bid *adieu* to my final D.C. friend last night. *Le sigh*. On Wednesday I welcome a group of 10 more lovelies. {Insert big smile}

This morning I settled in to send a stash of love notes {complete with Løv Organic tea bags secured by polka dot Japanese masking tape} before dashing off to a yoga class and tuning in to a Burda Style webinar on sewing later today.

I've been an avid purveyor of snail mail love notes since my early days. Mama Wilson would insist we pen holiday thank yous on Christmas day before we could play with said gifts. Also, my beloved Gramma and I had a letter-writing love affair for years. I especially smiled when she included stickers. And my passion for letting people know they are loved the old-fashioned way.

After my internship interview spring 2012, I followed up with a thank you note and tucked a tea bag inside. Before leaving my internship this spring, my supervisors confessed how "interesting" they found this tactic. Apparently it isn't common in the "real" world. So I made sure all notes to them came with tea bags moving forward and even attached one to my PowerPoint presentation in grad school last month. Again, probably not the norm.

Stationery brings *moi* great joy. I have an entire basket dedicated to blank cards waiting to find a home, stamps, and address labels. I also have another basket dedicated to mostly gifted blank journals waiting to be filled. Oh, and another basket or two with filled journals from bygone days. Plus a small box with tags, tiny gift cards, and confetti. Apparently stationery is an addiction to some and a love affair to others with various enabling websites, blogs, and forums. I think I'm somewhere in between. *Et toi?*

To ensure proper love notes continued while I was away, I toted 26 blank note cards and address labels with me to Paris. There is a feeling of extreme gratification when I stamp a love note and place it in the mailbox. A sort of knowing that it will be a welcomed surprise among bills, unwanted catalogs, and junk mail.

Pull out a colorful note card and let someone know you're thinking of them. Why not add a signature insert and seal it with a kiss? Snail mail is the new black.

8. UNPLUG
November 2013

Downtime is sacred. When asked what I did most of our recent Tranquility Tour, I giggle and confess that I, well, looked out the window. For hours. Days actually. And loved it.

In a culture that values productivity and making things happen, the notion of sitting fireside, strolling, or sipping tea at a sidewalk café for hours seems frivolous. The French refer to strolling as *flânerie* and it's a popular practice. Downtime may be just what the soul needs.

Stuck in an Internet connection haze while juggling reading a book last night, I came across a great article on 99u.com on the value of disconnecting. I had just led the mindfulness workshop at Tranquil Space earlier in the day where preaching meditation, unplugging, and deep thinking were part of the equation.

It was interesting to notice how feeling tired and ungrounded led me down a rabbit hole of switching from my book to quick peeks at my iPhone in search of additional stimulation. I mean, isn't a book enough? The only good part of last night's juggling moment is that I stumbled across the article and it hit a reset button of sorts. I copied the link, put down my iPhone, and couldn't wait to share it with you.

To summarize the article, here are the five suggestions for disconnected downtime:

1. **Create rituals for unplugging** {also on the *Tranquilologie* weekly checklist}

2. **Take daily doses of deep thinking** {maybe during your morning or evening routines}

3. **Try meditation and naps to clear the mind** {let this be your daily mindful movement}

4. **Consider self-awareness and psychological investment** {try exploratory journal writing}

5. **Protect the state of no-intent** {try this during your weekly soak in the tub}

Wishing you moments of mindful downtime. As we head into the hollydaze, we need these moments more than ever. Carve out some space. Disconnect. Whittle your commitments. Give the gift of your full presence.

> There is no better mental escape from our tech-charged world than the act of meditation.
> —Scott Belsky

9. TIME FOR WHAT MATTERS
December 2013

Since returning from the Tranquility Tour I've been doing lots of reflection on project creation, product enhancement, plus strategic use of time and energy coupled with what I most enjoy. You know, the ongoing dilemma you, too, may explore on a regular basis.

I created a visual plan and broke my life into five categories {four organizations + personal}. Using pink Post-it Notes and a Sharpie, I penned dreams {daily writing}, projects {*24 days o' Tranquility* e-course}, or plans {back patio garden} for the New Year. I also used larger Post-it Notes to highlight my love list {create, write, teach, travel, learn} and my most important list {teaching, learning, growing, creating, mindfulness, family time, making a difference}.

This process began as a Word document after settling back into life at the Pink Palace, but I don't want to have to open a document to view my dreams. So I pulled out cute Post-its and had a solo brainstorming session while also reviewing former years' dreams. I'll take the process further by crystallizing the dreams, penning the plans onto library cards, and inserting them into my *Daybook*.

Here are tips to make time for what matters in your life:

1. Ask yourself what you most love to do and jot it down. Put it someplace you'll see often.

2. Get clear on your most important overarching themes for the New Year. My 2014 theme is simplicity.

3. Break dreams into categories that resonate {products, projects, clients, etc.}.

4. Get clear on what resonates for 2014 fulfillment. Some dreams may be more long-term

{ex. grad school} and not doable in one year while others may be small to-dos {pen thank yous} that may not warrant their own Post-it.

5. Spend time with your *Daybook* penning your dreams or collaging them with images that represent what you want to bring forth.

6. Set timelines for your bigger projects or sign up for classes that will ensure you participate. For example, doing yoga or exercise at home may not be as successful as knowing you have a weekly date with your mat to keep you accountable.

7. Review these dreams weekly as you create your week's MITs {most important tasks} and try to take one tiny step daily to move closer to a dream or project fulfillment.

8. Get clear on how you're spending your 168 hours. How does this time usage align with your values? Where can you make adjustments to ensure your time supports your dreams?

Make time for what matters. You deserve it and so does this beautiful world awaiting your many gifts.

~ Reader Feedback ~

Kimberly's love affair with even the most simple things in life is absolutely contagious. Whether it's squealing over adorable potbelly pigs, musing on the latest must-read book, sharing her adventures from around the globe, or lovingly giving readers a peak into her heart, Kimberly repeatedly provides inspiration that helps readers become their best selves. As a long-time reader of *Tranquility du Jour* I can recollect how various posts have served as guideposts on my own life's journey.

Through Kimberly's writing, I have learned to live life deliberately, flairfully, and with intention. I have been inspired to live each moment with creativity and a style that's all my own. Whether learning how to select my clothing with care for daily dress up, carefully craft goals, engage in a restorative bed day, or how to dream up a glamorous morning routine, *Tranquility du Jour* has helped light the path of my self-discovery.

The way Kimberly bravely processed the loss of her beloved Gramma, with tremendous grace, honesty, and an open heart, helped guide me through the loss of my own best friend. The impact of her posts even traveled with me across the wide, sparkling ocean when her Parisian excursions inspired this fellow Francophile to take a solo-jaunt to Paris of my very own. I have tremendous gratitude for Kimberly. Kimberly's authenticity, presented in every post on *Tranquility du Jour*, beckons all readers to boldly live their own authentic lives. I'm certain this is true because her writing has impacted me to shed the "should be's" and to instead, simply live the sparkling truth of who I am. *Merci*, Kimberly!

Kylie Gretchen Howell, Alabama
makeitsomethingbeautiful.com

Anthology Extras: What Is Tranquility?
August 2013

During a recent writing workshop in Paris, I shared an excerpt from *Tranquilologie* and I noticed confused faces around the term "tranquility." To many, tranquility sounds like time at the spa, meditation in a remote setting, or escaping the day-to-day on a solo vacation.

Embracing tranquility while living a busy and full life is where it gets juicy. It's understandable to feel tranquil while on vacation or meditating away from everyday concerns. But finding tranquility "in the midst of rushing events," that's where the word comes alive. Thus, I've rewritten the definition to reflect my take on it as "the quality of calm within a full and meaningful life."

In *Living Your Yoga*, Judith Lasater explains practicing *pratyahara* {withdrawal of the senses and one of the eight limbs of yoga} as being in the middle of a busy marketplace and not affected by all that is going on around you. Think Black Friday at a big box store. You are centered and at peace even among chaos.

Next time you're in an overstimulating environment or rushing from A to B, stop, take a deep breath, and remember that tranquility can be yours. You have the choice to respond mindfully or react habitually. Keep this in mind while stuck in traffic or on a crowded beach this holiday weekend. Inhale, exhale.

Tranquility is: wrapping your hands around a warm cuppa tea, taking a deep breath in the midst of tension, saying what you mean and meaning what you say, feeling comfortable in your own skin, spending quality time with loved ones {*sans* smartphone}, living authentically, savoring a homemade meal, doing work that feels good, walking in the woods surrounded by fall foliage, getting clear on what you want, constantly learning, savoring a green juice, penning deep thoughts in a journal, feeling sunshine on your skin, stepping just outside your comfort zone, meeting a deadline with grace, pausing and doing a body scan.

Explore the quality of calm within your full and meaningful life. That's my definition of tranquility. Now tell me, what is tranquility to *you*?

> The very secret of life for me, I believed, was to maintain in the midst of rushing events an inner tranquility. —Margaret Bourke-White

10. BEGIN AGAIN
January 2014

The New Year is filled with a sense of possibility and, often, one too many resolutions. A focus on removing items from life can feel demoralizing {there's even a Say No to January campaign}. No more late nights. No more sugar. No more afternoon dates with the vending machine. No more running from appointment to appointment.

Consider reframing it around what you'd like to *add*. More joy. More downtime. More green juice. More yoga. More meditation. More family time. More whole foods. Psychologically, it can feel better to focus on what you'd like more of this year.

Although I love the process of reflecting and intention-setting, I appreciate the reminder in Sharon's quote that we can always begin again. So you met up with the vending machine after weeks of resisting and now feel you've ruined your New Year's plans. It's ok, you can start over.

Memoirist Dani Shapiro, author of *Still Writing*, writes, "Sharon Salzberg speaks of catching the mind scampering off, like the little monkey that it is, into the past, the future, anywhere but here, and suggests that the real skill in meditation is simply noticing that the mind has wandered. So liberating, this idea that we can start over at any time, a thousand times a day if need be."

Use January as a launching pad to live what you love, dabble in creating new habits, and constantly begin again. Creating sustainable shifts toward a more healthy, happy lifestyle takes time and energy. It will happen. And you deserve it.

> The amazing gift of being alive is that no matter what, we can always begin again.
> —Sharon Salzberg

LIFESTYLE NUGGETS

1. Take time for what matters.
2. Know you can always begin again.
3. Tranquility is a quality of calm within a full and meaningful life.

~ LIFESTYLE TAKEAWAYS ~

CHAPTER 5: Creativity

To be creative means to be in love with life. You can be creative only if you love life enough that you want to enhance its beauty, you want to bring a little more music to it, a little more poetry to it, a little more dance to it. —Osho

While sitting in an open-air art studio sprinkled with mosaics and glass hearts, I discovered the blending of paint, writing, and collage. This Mexico retreat imprinted happy art making on my soul. Painting a blank page, attaching images to that page, and then writing over the images offered a colorful and artistic spin to my journaling with a simple ballpoint pen onto lined paper. Wearing a vintage smock and playing in paint those few days opened up a new form of self-expression that has enhanced the way my words fill a page.

Over the past fifteen years I've been on a creative journey, courtesy of Julia Cameron's *The Artist's Way*. I have long credited her book to my launch of Tranquil Space and to my understanding that not just the Picassos of the world are artists. Although we may struggle to see ourselves as creative beings, we express our creativity in myriad ways every day: from the lip color we choose, to the food we consume, to the way we address our beloved.

In this compilation of blog posts you'll find encouragement to make small shifts, art journal, carry an ideas book, and keep the creative channels open. In addition, I share the story behind the creation of my clothing line and the pink planner, *Tranquility du Jour Daybook,* with hope of inspiring you to launch a creative endeavor of your own.

Tune into Tranquility du Jour podcasts #78, #235, #313 for more insights on creativity.

1. TRANQUILIT INSPIRATION
April 2005

Why TranquiliT? Who needs luxe yoga clothing? Why would one feel the need to feel fashionable while on the mat? The clothing line developed in the same way Tranquil Space began 5.5 years ago. There was not much yoga in D.C. and I craved a like-hearted community. So I set out to create someplace special for others to be inspired where tea and cookies would be served to complete their experience.

TranquiliT grew out of my need to feel less frumpy while living in yoga wear seven days a week. When I began teaching yoga full-time and subbed downtown, I felt uncomfortable in my black leggings and t-shirt surrounded by professionals in business attire. But who has time to change clothes simply to walk to the next class to teach across town?

I began adding a skirt over my yoga pants so I didn't feel as exposed, but that didn't quite solve my unease. I've always found that when I present my best self outwardly, I feel better inwardly. This relates to my practice too. When I am in comfortable clothing that I can easily wear on and off the mat, I transition easily from meetings to the café to yoga practice. Thus, TranquiliT was born.

Are you seeking something more in your life? Do you think that you may have ideas that can solve a problem for yourself and others? Maybe a motivational book club with your besties? How about a functional AND fashionable bag that actually fits everything you need to carry? Or a book that shares your life journey and will inspire others?

Now is the time to create. Your challenges or needs are probably faced by others, too. Risk taking and attention to your own needs may just lead others to a Tranquil Space or to don a dose of TranquiliT.

2. SMALL SHIFTS
February 2010

Today was yummy. After shipping TranquiliT online orders into the wee hours and curling up with *The Not So Big Life* yesterday, I did my best to nurture my creative and spiritual side today.

The day began with a jaunt to Le Pug's fave pet store for oodles of organic treats. They asked if it was his birthday. "Oh, no, he had a sprained toe last week!" I replied. The ladies at the counter gave me one of *those* looks.

Then I organized *chez moi* for a couple of hours. It's amazing how a little shuffling of items can make such a difference. I emptied two boxes of my yoga CDs into a clear bin, tossed a broken candleabra, and put *Tranquilista* books into a cute basket rather than the drab cardboard box they arrived in. Swept the floor, washed counters, and organized my tea shelf. Minor shifts are refreshing.

Next, off to yummy yin yoga at Tranquil Space where I met up with a dear friend. Back to *chez moi* for creative play and catch up. After dinner she headed home, and I continued to create in front of the fire while listening to a meditation CD by Tara Brach.

What small shifts can you take to refresh your spirit? Dust a shelf. Write in your journal. Send a love note. Bake cookies. Clean out your linen closet. Sleep in. Read *The New York Times*. Collage. Take a technology fast. Donate books, clothes, or toiletries.

Here's to continued small shifts and happy spirits.

> What small shifts can you make to refresh your spirit?

3. IDEAS BOOK
May 2010

In addition to my journal and planner, I like to carry an ideas book to capture inspiration on-the-go. I've recently added layers to it—similar to a visual journal—and now paste ideas inside rather than simply writing them.

The addition of a colorful Juicy Couture ad over the flocked damask cover has been eye candy for my soul. Inside my ideas book you'll find:

Biz cards of fabulous places/people

Blog post ideas

Books I find on shelves that I *must* have

Authors or websites I come across and want to research further

Decor tips from swanky cafés, boutiques, and yoga studios

Inspiration gathered from a meeting or book

Random to-do ideas that come to me during a workshop

Notes from workshops, classes, or conferences

I store my ideas book upon completion and go through them occasionally. Most last a year or so before they are filled and need to be replaced. It's fun to note how many of the ideas are implemented, authors are contacted, books are read, and inspirations are savored.

Do you carry an ideas book? If so, what does it contain? If not, pick up a tiny Moleskine this week and watch what unfolds. Fill it with recipes, advice, favorite quotes, tips from magazines, dreams, drawings, and more. It's a tiny creative container for your future projects.

4. ART JOURNALING
January 2011

Art journal:
A way to give physical form to your thoughts, everyday events, and dreams.

Types of art journals:
Daily thoughts, travel journal, exercise diary, diet diary, dream journal, business plan, goals, to-dos or ideas, cards, any record that you'd like to keep in a book or notebook.

How to:
Gather images, words, photos, paint, markers, journal, paper bags, tissue paper, scissors, glue sticks, Japanese masking tape, favorite magazines, stamps, stamp pads, ribbon, and other ephemera. Open to any page, provide background, add images, add writing, date. *Voilà*!

Why:
Because it's fun, involves reused materials, and fuels your creative spark! And regular practice of creating via an art journal "can reduce your heart rate, increase serotonin flow and immune cells, and decrease stress responses," according to Elizabeth Warson of George Washington University's Art Therapy program. Her findings complement James Pennebaker's studies on the benefits of writing about distressful experiences, and the physiological changes that journaling can bring about in the long term.

~ Reader Feedback ~

In the fall of 2005 I began my dream job at a record label just outside of Nashville, TN. With the job came a forty-five minute commute, and I found the *Hip Tranquil Chick* podcast. I think I started around episode 25 or so, and quickly downloaded all of the back catalogue. The creativity that I had pushed down during four years of business school was reignited.

The job didn't work out. The music industry was in the middle of its transformation and it wasn't an environment I enjoyed being in. However, I did have a lot of time to read the blog. Inspired by Kimberly's story, I began teaching Pilates, painting, and writing. I enrolled in her online Creativity Circle the year my daughter was born and wrote a novella the following year. Even when I chose to go back into the corporate workforce, creativity, entrepreneurship and spiritual balance remained life goals, supported by the blog and podcasts.

I continued to teach Pilates and, inspired by idea of a "yoga lifestyle" I wrote *Your Pilates Life*, a book about how integrating the Pilates Principles into everyday life could help inspire creativity, mindfulness, and health. I enrolled in a creative writing program at a local college and have written four novels. One of which has been published and one is coming out in December. With the help of my husband, I am raising two awesome kids, two dogs and working on my master's in fine arts in creative writing. I continue to turn to *Tranquility du Jour* for inspiration nearly every day, and am so thankful for the virtual guidance Kimberly has shared.

Thanks, Kimberly, for ten awesome years. Here's to ten more.

Amanda Michelle Moon, Minnesota
amandamichellemoon.com

~ Reader Feedback ~

Kimberly and *Tranquility du Jour* have given me the key to open up my own creativity and self-expression, and have inspired me as a leader in so many ways.

The blog has been like having my own Google alert on all things tranquil—delivering inspiration and tips that are not just relevant to me, but touch my soul and inspire me to go deeper, feel more, and find my grace in the busyness of life. It's comforting to have a place to come home to, a safe haven, where you can snuggle up and be inspired by insights and suggestions to live a more tranquil life.

In the very beginning, following Kimberly's journey in publishing *Hip Tranquil Chick* inspired me to publish my first book. I continued to soak up the posts and ponder, "What can I take from these insights for my life?" The blog has led me to some of my greatest mentors, books, business insights, and daily reminders to live more mindfully. Thank you!

Kristi Daniels, California
kristidaniels.com

5. AU REVOIR SQUAM
September 2011

Filled with gratitude for the chance to spend a few days focused on creativity at the Squam Art Retreat in New Hampshire. Definitely an area beckoning more attention from me {versus so much admin time}. Seems to be a common struggle, eh?

The thing about creativity is it isn't a luxury; it's a necessity. Incorporating it every day is essential. An annual retreat is not enough.

This week, try to do one creative expression each day: take a photo on the way to work, stick a love note in your child's lunchbox, wear a new shade of lip gloss, try a new *parfum*, create a collage or a vision board, pick up a new pair of earrings from a street vendor, try yin yoga, wear red, listen to a podcast, sip a blooming tea, meditate, plant mums, pull out your fall wardrobe and retire flip flops, go to an art exhibit, put up art postcards in your cubicle, peruse Etsy, sit under a tree, pen your thoughts.

May we continue to explore and become the people we were born to be.

6. LET YOUR LIFE SHINE
October 2011

A new favorite motto is "let your life shine." But what does it mean? How can one let their life shine? The phrase brings me back to Sunday school days of singing *This little light of mine, I'm gonna let it shine*. Remember that song? Catchy tune! Well, I simply replaced light with life and, *voilà*, I have a new motto. Here are a few simple ways to let your life shine:

- Pen your thoughts
- Express yourself through movement
- Think BIG
- Be an activist
- Do privately what you preach publicly

- Pursue your passion
- Dive into your dreams
- Let go
- Take the high road
- Live beautifully
- Heal old hurts
- Smile at strangers

- Give back
- Honor all beings
- Don sparkles
- Light candles
- Savor simplicity
- Sprinkle magic

Et toi? How do you believe we can let our lives shine?

7. ARTIST DATE NEW YORK
March 2012

After an exciting showing of the documentary *Vegucated* at Tranquil Space last night, Le Beau and I chatted into the wee hours discussing heaps of ideas and rehashing the past two weeks. Last I recall, the clock glared 12:30 a.m. Then the alarm sang at 4:30 a.m. {yikes!}. I jumped out of bed and onto a bus to NYC. Shocked to find a full bus, I napped a bit sitting straight up en route to Holly Becker's blogging workshop. Hmmm, can we say tired?

I was delighted to be greeted with such beauty at the workshop: colorful journals for note taking, a small ephemera packet, handmade banners hung throughout, vibrant tulips, pastel paper goods, and pussy willows donning tied ribbons. I immediately felt at home.

I took 10 pages of notes in my tiny ideas book, and wanted to share a few takeaways in no particular order:

- use your blog as a catalyst to live your best life
- be an explorer of the world—see things with new eyes
- craft mood boards {an arrangement of images, materials, and text intended to evoke a concept}
- read *The Accidental Creative*
- read + comment on other blogs
- ask others what they see your strengths + weaknesses to be
- ask yourself lots of questions
- note five major goals you want to achieve
- weed your garden {literally + figuratively}
- have dinner alone
- answer, "if you had all the resources in the world, what would you be doing with your life?"
- write weekly columns
- try a six-week series
- do regular blog redesigns
- do a blog survey
- post regularly on where else you can be found {ex. Twitter, Facebook}
- host a pop-up shop = love!
- host blog sponsors
- teach workshops, online courses, classes
- sell downloadable content and products
- CAKE = confident, approachable, knowledgeable, engaging
- answer, "what story do you want your blog to tell?"
- showcase most popular posts
- have a clear about + contact page

Fun stuff, eh? Considering I've been blogging for nearly seven years now, it's amazing how much there is still to learn and experience. The incorporation of photos plus the beauty of Instagram {@Tranquilitydujour} has added such a creative touch to *Tranquility du Jour*. Instagram turns the smartphone and everyday adventures into art.

I hope this Artist Date sprinkles some love into your blogging or journaling journey. Wishing you a tranquil Saturday night. I'm off to do a few moments of window shopping before busing back to D.C.

If you have any suggestions for *Tranquility du Jour*, please pass them along as I love all your fun ideas and many things have come out of them such as *Tranquilologie, Tranquility du Jour Daybook,* and the *Creative + Conscious Business* e-course!

Anthology Extras: Joy of Journaling
June 2011

Last night I brought my latest journal to a close. It always feels cathartic, and a bit sad, to pen final thoughts in a journal. It's as if that chapter is over and I'm moving on despite having it documented and at my fingertips. Sigh. However, the joy of starting fresh is all-too-exciting—especially with this gorgeous Papaya Art journal.

A few favorite journaling tips:

1. Write as the muse hits.
2. Writing first thing in the morning can be a great brain dump extravaganza.
3. Note date, time, location, mood.
4. Ponder, "What isn't working?" or "What wants attention?" or "What is transpiring within?"
5. Doodle, dream, draft.
6. Add color: pens, paint, markers.
7. Explore themes.
8. Forgo punctuation, grammar, spelling.
9. Keep your journal in tow, especially on travels.
10. Let go of your inner critic.

8. $100 PROJECT
December 2012

I received $100 at the World Domination Summit to "start a project, surprise someone, or do something entirely different." Today I'm excited to share how I've invested the $100 combined with few thousand more, hours of creating, editing, prepping, and soon-to-be shipping.

As a passionate planner and connoisseur of organizational tools, pals have encouraged me to create a sort of pink planner pad with girly flair. And on December 22, 2009, I received an email from an online pal, Britt Bravo, with the following:

I know you don't need any more ideas {!}, but I was doing some research this morning for a blog post about calendars published by non-profits, and it occurred to me that you would be the perfect person to create a calendar or day planner, with photos, quotes, reflection questions, petals, etc., about women, yoga, creativity and leadership, and part of the profits of the calendar's sales could go to Tranquil Space Foundation.

Clearly a seed was planted because after months of behind the scenes work, on November 11, 2012, I launched pre-sale of the *Tranquility du Jour Daybook*. This past Friday Britt reminded me of this email. When I reviewed it, I was surprised to see how many pieces made it into the *Daybook* despite not having laid eyes on the email for nearly three years. Ah, synchronicity!

Somehow the pieces all came together. I created the daily, weekly, and monthly checklists plus weekly planner layout for *Tranquilologie* earlier this year and wanted to design a sweet complementary companion.

> What would you do with $100 and a dream?

Artist and friend Mary Catherine Starr created beautiful watercolors of my favorite things. Coupled with a talented graphic designer, Christy, and editor extraordinaire, Carol, I have been blessed with an amazing team throughout the process.

I added seasonal wheels of life, blank pages for collage, note taking, or doodling, signature savvy sources, and a table of contents for easy access to all the inner gems.

The *Daybooks* shipped yesterday and are en route to *moi*. Upon receipt in the next few days, I'll be packing them with lots of love and sending them right out to you! This little elf has been wrapping baker's twine around pink tags, prepping the darling stickers and appointment cards, and gathering all the accessories to make the *Daybook* a source of grand inspiration for your upcoming year.

Trust that seeds are constantly planted. Although they may not take root immediately, creativity is stirring below the surface. Give your dreams time, water, fertile soil, and adequate sun to sprout.

What would you do with $100 and a dream?

9. DAY WITH JULIA CAMERON
December 2012

On Saturday fellow creativity seeker, Carol, picked me with my thermos of green tea in hand up at 4:45 a.m. After scintillating early morning conversation, we boarded a bus en route to NYC at 5:15 a.m. Considering I've been preaching the gospel of *The Artist's Way* for well over a decade, I decided it was time to meet the master. At 10 a.m. I arrived at Open Center with smeared lipstick across my face {thanks to head bobbing bus slumbering}, a hungry belly {quickly healed with kale chips + dried mango}, and no eye makeup. Despite feeling like a hot mess, I was giddy with excitement about what was to come—once I removed the misplaced red lipstick and added signature cat eyes.

The day was filled with exercises from her books. Many I've done over the years and some new ones. One thing I enjoyed was the focus on creating action steps around what we were seeking. The biggest resistance for *moi* came up around constantly finding clusters of three new people to work with and share. I'm okay for a few sharing sessions, but the day was packed with them. As an introvert, being forced into small talk is challenging. I put on my big girl pants and only escaped to the loo during one sharing session. I mean, sometimes a girl's gotta go . . . or avoid.

Exercises found in my sparkly pink idea book:

1. Fill in the blank: artists are X

2. List five imaginary lives and five actions to get you closer to them

    Mine = burlesque dancer, documentary maker, watercolor painter, memoirist, philanthropist

3. 15 things that make you happy

4. Five things you love

    Mine = feeling appreciated, learning, making a difference, French chic style, travel

5. Answer: what do you need to know? What do you need to do? What do you need to try? What do you need to accept?

    Mine = how not to let things get to me so intensely; yoga, yoga, yoga; dancing/performance; not sure

6. Rate these areas of your life {think Wheel of Life}: spirituality, exercise, play, work, friends, romance/adventure and list one action to enhance each category

7. Rate areas of your body and list one action to improve the area

8. Rate areas of your home and list one action to improve the area

9. Fill in the blank: if you didn't have to do it perfectly, you'd try X

    Mine = create a documentary, watercolor, draw, burlesque dancing, have a fashion truck, host meetups, host a NYC workshop

10. Fill in the blank: you'd love to X

    Mine = travel, find spaciousness, feel inner peace, save farm animals, write a memoir

11. List five ways you are mean to yourself

12. List five actions to be kinder to yourself

    Mine = schedule weekly Artist Dates; write Morning Pages; prioritize exercise + self-care; get up earlier/to bed earlier; digital time off

13. Explore creative U-turns in music, writing, dance, visual arts, cooking, size of personality, theater, public speaking, photography, film

14. Fill in the blank: an adventure you'd love to have is X

    Mine = traveling cross-country in an Airstream, setting up a fashion truck, having a piglet

15. Five things you really love doing

16. Five characteristics you want in a creativity god

17. Pen a note to your creativity god on where you are and where you need help

18. Pen note back to self from creativity god

After the session, I walked to Jivamukti café with Carol for some tasty vegan food, got my yoga on, and dashed to the 9 p.m. bus home with my pink thermos topped up with chamomile tea. I'm still processing the experience and look forward to doing heaps of reflection during the hollydaze on 2012, dreams for 2013, and some of the action steps that came out of this workshop. Try some of them yourself and let *moi* know what comes up for you.

10. KEEP THE CHANNEL OPEN
May 2014

Bonjour from the tropics where my downtime is spent writing, editing, and getting bodywork on my injured joints. Before I settle in to work on penning the intro to my upcoming *Anthology*, I wanted to check in with you, my dear reader.

Last night while leading a writing workshop for our retreaters, I shared the ways yoga and writing align, tools for the writing practice, and various prompts. In addition, I introduced the quote by Martha Graham that is a critical reminder to the creative process. Here it is:

There is a vitality, a life force, a quickening that is translated through you into action, and because there is only one of you in all time, this expression is unique. And if you block it, it will never exist through any other medium and be lost. The world will not have

it. It is not your business to determine how good it is, nor how valuable it is, nor how it compares with other expressions. It is your business to keep it yours clearly and directly, to keep the channel open. You do not even have to believe in yourself or your work. You have to keep open and aware directly to the urges that motivate YOU. Keep the channel open.

I'd like to remind you, too, that what you have to share with the world is important. And it takes practice. And it takes time. And it takes energy. And it takes vulnerability. And it takes being a beginner. And it takes perseverance. And, frankly, it takes chutzpah.

Stay present and watch what flows. We want to see, hear, smell, taste, and feel it. No one else can offer what you do. Keep the channel open.

CREATIVITY NUGGETS

1. Tote an ideas book to capture inspiration in the moment.

2. Small shifts can lead to big change.

3. Keep your creative channel open.

~ CREATIVITY TAKEAWAYS ~

CHAPTER 6: Entrepreneurship

If you cannot do great things, do small things in a great way. —Napoleon Hill

We're discussing the decor, entertainment, and treats for the upcoming 15th year birthday bash of my firstborn entrepreneurial baby, Tranquil Space. Damask, white lights, macarons, a female DJ, a talk or two, and a champagne flute takeaway are feeling like a festive celebration.

The years have been fraught with hard decisions, long hours, and a continual shift between the left and right brain. I've learned to tackle tough issues with as much grace as possible. I've felt nauseous in my belly when personally guaranteeing a $350,000 SBA loan to cover build-out costs on a new location. I've been able to hand over high-level operations and trust a talented team to carry out the vision.

It hasn't been easy, yet I can't imagine my 20s, 30s, and early 40s any different. In *Tranquilista* I noted how we're all entrepreneurs of our own lives. Yep, you read it right, no business necessary. An entrepreneur is defined as "a person who organizes and manages any enterprise, especially a business, usually with considerable initiative and risk." Life is an enterprise and we each manage our own. Some days are a little better than others.

In this chapter you'll find stories about Tranquil Space and TranquiliT, a peek at a day in the life, a breakdown of the tasks that make up running varied businesses, a piece on feeling untapped, and more.

Tune into *Tranquility du Jour* podcasts #175, #244, #314 for more insights on entrepreneurship.

1. CREATION OF TRANQUIL SPACE
December 2004

As we journey into the last month of 2004, let's reflect on the year's lessons and stories, as well as the vision of Tranquil Space with a focus on creatively humble beginnings. Tranquil Space began a little over five years ago in my one-bedroom apartment on the outskirts of Washington, D.C.'s Dupont Circle neighborhood. There was little yoga in the area. It was an edgy thing to do, not receiving the interest of today. I was working as a paralegal, reading *The Artist's Way* and seeking a more creative way of life. Longing for kindred spirits and hoping that they existed in D.C. But where to find them?

With visions of strangers huddled around my fireplace, drinking tea, doing yoga and connecting, I began hanging fliers around Dupont Circle. This was a BIG step, I realize it now, but it felt so natural at the time. Inviting strangers into one's living room isn't a habit I recommend, but my faith in the practice of yoga, and my desire for community necessitated it. I continued to surprise myself along the way: the joy that brewing a homemade batch of chai for every class brought, the excitement of watching students' eyes light up when they blossomed into a pose, the pleasure yoga was bringing to people who met through class, and the love I felt for the business.

With a psychology degree and no business training, I began with a focus on the special details: ribbons wrapped around inspirational quotes to greet students on their mat, aromatic scents, a blazing fire, chai served in porcelain tea cups, homemade business cards and brochures. I put time into making people feel special because it's often lacking in our fast-paced society. I wanted students to walk into class and feel welcomed and accepted, not judged. I especially wanted

> Life shrinks or expands in proportion to one's courage.
> — Anaïs Nin

women to find a safe space to work with their bodies, develop a sense of empowerment, and explore taking steps towards their idealized life. Thus Tranquil Space began.

We have grown 1000% over the past five years and I am constantly amazed by the sacred souls I've met which would never have happened had I not hung up that first neighborhood flier. The reason I started the studio has been an important reflection of mine over the past few months as we hit our fifth year. I'd woven together trunk shows, feminine studio décor, lifestyle-focused off the mat workshops, boutique, new studio expansion, TranquiliT clothing designs, various charities, greening efforts, and writing, I wanted to explore how my initial reason for starting the studio was expanding.

One may have trouble seeing how all of these components are connected, but I'm hopeful my philosophy and reason for developing Tranquil Space helps to clarify. I truly believe that yoga for the sake of yoga is powerful, but not as powerful as sprinkling it throughout one's lifestyle. Yoga serves as my catalyst, my core, that place I turn to when my world is spinning. I was drawn to it for the healing powers that it provided mentally, physically, and emotionally.

Yoga offers an opportunity to spend time connecting to the body, surrendering the mind, pushing edges of comfort, and honoring limitations. Knowing how much better I feel when I'm comfortably put together, I sought stretchy clothing perfect for yogis to our unique boutique, and created our own collection. The trunk shows offer female artists a chance to showcase their creativity.

How many of us say, "Oh, I'd love to do such and such but now just isn't the right time"? NOW is the time to begin taking steps to create what you desire. Social consciousness has always been an important component to me with the numerous charities we support: Washington Humane Society, Arbor Day Foundation, and My Sister's Place. And the focus on greening Tranquil Space aligns with *ahimsa* {non-harming}—treating the environment consciously. The off the mat workshops help to teach students how to live their lives mindfully. All of these random parts blend to form the focus of Tranquil Space.

My hope is that Tranquil Space serves as an inspiration to anyone who enters its doors. It was created with a whole lot of love, no business experience, an incredible amount of time, energy and passion, and LOTS of baby steps. I truly believe and hope to embody Anaïs Nin's above quote. Life is lived by stepping strategically outside of one's comfort zone to head in the direction of one's dreams. This direction is not without mistakes, drama, or sometimes failure, but it is filled with authenticity because you are DOING, along with dreaming. Sarah Breathnach, author of *Simple Abundance*, states, "The world needs dreamers and the world needs doers, but above all the world needs dreamers who do."

May the end of 2004 offer you some time to reflect on what it is you want to create—a family, a perfume, a book, a movement—whatever it is, listen to your heart and take steps heading in that direction, even if it's only one flier at a time.

2. JOY OF FULL BLOOM
October 2005

I'm writing to share a gentle reminder that effort pays off, even if it takes time to come to fruition.

I've been working on a book blending yoga and lifestyle for the modern girl, and this week I received offers from publishers. I came up with the concept two years ago, took a great "how to get published class," worked on the proposal for almost a year during any spare moment {namely vacations}, submitted it to targeted agents, got a fabulous agent last October, finished my sample chapter in June, and submitted the package to publishers in July. Whew!

We've received great feedback, especially on presentation. For example, I tied a ribbon around the portfolio, added a bag of tea, used heavy paper, added personalized labels onto colored tabs to identify the appendices, and inserted splashes of color wherever I could. The result was a proposal that looked and smelled different from others.

I share this because it has been a long journey and it has only just begun. Once an offer is accepted, I have six to nine months to write the book with hopes of getting it into the market for holiday 2006. Can you believe we're preparing

for holiday 2006? Dreams are truly a long time coming. When all is said and done, this will have been a four-year project.

The dream began as a little girl falling asleep to the sound of my father's typewriter. I grew up surrounded by the writer's life and somehow envied the isolation, deadlines, creative juice, and long hours. Let the writing begin . . . and thank you for your support by reading this blog.

I'm also delighted to share that the TranquiliT line will be featured in this weekend's *Examiner*. This creative journey began in 2002, and took new life in 2004 as I began drawing, designing more, traveling to tradeshows, and choosing fabrics. It, too, has been a long process of workshops, sewing classes, reading trade publications, putting together a design board with fabric swatches and style ideas, locating manufactures, selling the line for 12 hours at tradeshows, photo shoots, line sheet designs, working with the webmaster on creating an online store, choosing the right tags and labels, putting together spec sheets, and writing press releases. It's amazing what goes into launching a line. And it's so rewarding to see people excited to wear something you've created.

Remember, it often takes years to see the fruits of your labor. Think of yourself as a seed germinating below the surface and each step you take {research, classes, travel} offers you the opportunity to water and nurture yourself into full bloom.

~ Reader Feedback ~

Impact is defined as the powerful effect that something has on somebody or something. Measuring impact is complex, but as I reflect on my life since stumbling across *Tranquility du Jour* and Kimberly Wilson, I can see the unmistakable influence of this blog.

July 2006, I was packing for a plane trip to Bulgaria. Browsing iTunes I stumbled across a podcast called *Hip Tranquil Chick*. I was neither 'hip' nor 'tranquil' but as a 'chick' I was intrigued and downloaded seven podcasts to my white iPod {remember those?}. Listening to the narration, whilst the clouds floated by, I became hooked. The topic areas resonated loudly with me: yoga and a modern lifestyle, soulful surroundings, living authentically, self-care tips, and reading recommendations. This material kept me company on the trip and I was desperate to log on at home to explore the accompanying blog.

Over the years I have listened to the podcasts, devoured the blog, and have been on a continuous learning journey. The real impact for me was when in 2008, I signed up for an associated e-course during a course of fertility treatment. As a control freak, Type A personality I was instructed by my medical team to slow down, relax and shift my focus. With forced time away from my work, I threw myself into the course material and used the suggested breathing exercises to get me through the many tests and procedures a fertility journey flings at you.

At the end of the course, as well as being equipped with a fresh outlook on life, I was also pregnant with twins {now 5 years of age}. Those breathing skills and the associated focus were imperative during such a taxing time {and also during toddler tantrums!}, and I will always be indebted to you. In addition, you've made me realize that the little things in life, for example fresh flowers, being totally present, handwritten notes, a special glass of champagne, are actually the significant things. Thank you for giving me the skills to hit pause and appreciate the precious silence amongst the noise.

Alison Day, England
www.alison-day.com

3. A DAY IN THE LIFE
February 2006

Recently I put together a day in the life schedule of my world for a women's entrepreneurial case study. I was asked to categorize "B" for business and "P" for personal. After putting this together I realized that the two were so intertwined that it would be impossible. I love my work and live what I do, so it is hard to distinguish the two. Not sure if this is good or completely imbalanced, but somehow it works for me right now. I work constantly and LOVE what I do.

Considering I find it insightful to see how others live and balance various things, I thought I would share this with you. Have you ever put together a day in the life of your world? Right now mine is very writing-focused but this changes once deadlines are met. Also, I find comparing an actual and an ideal schedule enlightening. This helps highlight how they differ and then I'll explore what small changes can be made to bring them closer into alignment.

M–F

9:00 a.m.: Rise and shine, check email and handle urgent matters, make green tea, walk Le Pug

10:00 a.m. to noon: Dive into email, respond, check in with studio, eat breakfast, shower, write or meetings with staff, consultants, or business allies

Noon to 5:00 p.m.: Write, more meetings, email responses, team updates, possibly head to studio, PR work, clothing line efforts, meeting with manager on studio operations and projects, lunch while working

5:00 p.m. to 9:00 p.m.: Take and teach yoga classes, work at studio

9:00 p.m. to midnight: Blog, write, read, email responses, meetings with consultants, eat dinner, date with Le Beau or friends one night a week, take hot bath

Saturday

10:00 a.m.: Rise and shine, check email and handle urgent matters, make green tea, shower

11:30 a.m.: Head to studio

Noon: Take class

1:30 p.m.: Teach class

3:00 p.m. to 6:00 p.m.: Meetings on projects with consultants or team

6:00 p.m. to 1 a.m.: Write, blog, read, take hot bath, dinner date with Le Beau or friends

Sunday

10:00 a.m. to noon: Rise and shine, check email and handle urgent matters, make green tea, writing

Noon-1:00 a.m.: Varies. Typically this day is spent away from the studio writing, running studio or personal errands, writing podcast show notes, podcasting, posting podcast show notes, responding to weekly studio wrap-up, planning next week's priorities, emails, occasional hosting of outside workshops or trunk shows, meetings regarding clothing line

For a current peek into "Day in the Life," refer to p. 190.

TOP FIVE BUSINESS TIPS

I was recently interviewed for a podcast where the host asked me my top 5 business tips so I pulled these together to share:

1. Start small, grow organically.
2. Focus on creating an experience.
3. Be the brand—eat, sleep, live it.
4. Seek balance.
5. Set an intention.

> The greatest achievement was at first and for a time a dream. The oak sleeps in the acorn, the bird waits in the egg, and in the highest vision of the soul a waking angel stirs. Dreams are the seedlings of realities. —James Allen

4. A NEW TRANQUIL SPACE
December 2007

Happy almost 2008! A new year, a new Tranquil Space. I am very excited to share that this spring we will open our doors at 17th and R in a newly renovated and eco-fabulous Tranquil Space. It's been hard to keep this to myself as I'm bursting at the seams with delight. After planting the seeds in my living room on 16th street in 1999, offering classes in a church parlor for almost three years at 16th and Q, and then moving to our current location on P Street, I am honored to be returning to our neighborhood roots after over a year of searching for the perfect tranquil space.

Your new yoga home will house three yoga studios, an expanded boutique, and a specialty spa. When I signed the dotted line, there were broken windows and pigeons living in the space. It has taken a lot of vision to see the possibility amidst the leaking roof, sunlight peeping through neglected bricks, and roots growing within the water lines of this three-story building. As the space gets framed and we receive permits, buy reused fixtures, design the layout, and choose the eco-friendly flooring, it's slowly taking shape.

May 2008 offer you time to reflect on your vision. What are your dreams for 2008? What will you do to make them happen? Listen to your heart and take the simple steps of heading in that direction. I can't wait to practice with you in our new home when the cherry blossoms are in bloom.

> Listen to your heart and take the simple steps of heading in that direction.

5. WHAT DO YOU DO?
February 2010

This question has been a challenge for the past decade. Especially when I first started teaching yoga and the whole concept was less accepted than it is now. I've been a consultant {fancy word for yoga teacher accepted by Washingtonians}, a yoga teacher {didn't cover everything else I did when not teaching yoga}, a yoga studio owner {I don't simply own a studio, I *work* at a studio}. Hmmm, never quite found the right response to this question. Thus, I came up with "yogini, teacher, entrepreneur, do-gooder, author, eco-designer" to describe myself in a nutshell. What do you say to this sure-to-be-asked cocktail party question?

During my time in Mexico last month I took a crack at writing what I did and wanted to share my list in case it would provide insights into running two yoga studios {Tranquil Space, TS}, a clothing line {TranquiliT, TT}, non-profit {Tranquil Space Foundation, TSF}, and lifestyle company {Hip Tranquil Ventures, HTV}. I included additional pieces as KW.

Initiate content and ideas for promos and eblasts: TT, TSF, HTV, TS

Write muse for newsletter: HTV, TS, TSF

Pay bills: TT, TSF, HTV, TS

Create meeting agendas: TSF, TS

Design clothing: TT

Schedule/plan photo shoots: TT, TS

Review/approve samples: TT

Cultivate experience: TT, TSF, HTV, TS

Lead retreats: HTV, TS

Initiate content and interviews for podcasts/videos: HTV

Ship orders: HTV, TT

Oversee schedules: TS

Team management: TS, TT, TSF

Oversee teacher training with director: TS

Media interviews: TT, HTV, TS, TSF

Host/develop team retreats: TS

Register/prep/tend booth at tradeshows: TT

Social work degree: KW

Collaborate with accountant: TS, TSF, HTV, TT

Teach at Kripalu: HTV

Manage bank accounts + send detailed data to accountant monthly: TS, TSF, HTV, TT, KW

Social media: TT, TS, HTV, TSF

Run online ecourses: HTV

Oversee web redesigns/edits: TT, TS, HTV, TSF

Choose, order, count inventory: TT

Oversee boutique with manager: TS

Blog posts: TS, HTV

Write articles + guest posts: HTV

Teach workshops + teacher training: TS

Travel teaching: HTV

Marketing: TS, TSF, HTV, TT

Work with vendors {printing, fabric, trim, photographers, seamstress}: TS, TSF, HTV, TT

Schedule + manage/assist events: TS, HTV, TT, TSF

Schedule + host seasonal teleclasses: HTV

Design + produce gemstone necklaces: TT

Choose + purchase team gifts: TS, TSF

Send happy birthday notes to team: TS, TSF

Hire, oversee, post guest bloggers: HTV

Sewing for launch of Etsy store: KW

Collaborate with fellow femmes on new events: HTV

Lead team meetings: TS, TSF

Handle official docs {trademarks, LLCs, agreements}: TSF, TS, HTV, TT

Strategic planning: TSF, TS, HTV, TT

Engage in professional development: TT, TSF, HTV, TS

When I wrote this out, it was eye-opening. Ever feel like you do, do, do and at the end of the day your to-do list is still a mile long? My plan is to start keeping a record of how my time is spent {if you work as a consultant or in the legal world you may do this}.

Get clear on what you do to make sure you infuse your world with as much of what you love to do as possible. So, tell me, what do *you* do?

6. NEW YOGA HOME
August 2010

Tranquil Space Arlington's new home opened last night. Woo-hoo! The journey began in 2007 when we opened within a dance studio {similar to our church days for Dupont}. Quickly recognizing that we needed more space and the ability to control the environment {dance music + *savasana* ≠ tranquility}, we began looking for the perfect spot.

2008 was focused on moving into our 17th street location so a 2009 move was the plan for Arlington. However, we began looking mid-2008 on and had many deals fall through. Yet we persevered. The Arlington community needed a home of their own.

One sad January day—coined National Yoga Day—we had a meeting with our Arlington front desk staff, welcomed arriving yogis to a sold-out class with an influx of newbies on this discounted day, and set off to look at lots of available spaces with our contractor. None was a match. Sigh. Yep, *this* is how I spend my Saturdays.

As we passed the cute space currently housing a Curves franchise, I said to Le Beau and our contractor, "If only that space was available, it would be perfect!" It was sweet with a little lawn, parking in the back, and a stand alone building—no neighbors above or below. Seemed like a true home. A little over a year later, we signed the lease. The for lease sign went up last summer and we negotiated for almost a year.

Last night, we opened our doors to welcome our patient, loyal, loving community into their new Tranquil Space. It meant so much to me because I know what they've put up with over the years {e.g. some of you may remember the days of being in *savasana* during wedding processions at the 16th Street church} when many conditions were beyond our control.

We've added special Tranquil Space touches: body products in both loos, individual changing stalls complete with velvet curtains, tea and cookies outside the studio, a spacious sitting area and retail space, chandeliers to add sparkle, damask to add flair, green touches to honor the environment, and complimentary mints everywhere.

This story is the perfect reminder that patience prevails. There were many times when we got close to signing a lease and something fell through that I wondered if it was a sign. Yet, I knew in my heart that the community we planted in 2007 across the river deserved a practice space that offered them a chance to bloom.

And you know what? The yogis were abuzz last night and our new home has wonderful energy. Perfect for blooming!

Anthology Extras: TranquiliT Showroom
July 2008

During the E-Myth {my favorite business book} Conference in California, I decided it was time to move TranquiliT into its own home—it deserves it. I found a darling place nearby and am finalizing logistics now. I'm hopeful it happens as I look forward to launching this baby into its own. Will keep you posted as my fingers are crossed and I'm excited about possibility.

In the interim, life has been a bit of a zoo since my return. Although I'm able to stay in touch and on top of things fairly well while away {due to the beauty of wireless Internet}, there are usually more balls in the air despite best laid plans upon return.

Details, details, details. There is a great quote by Thoreau about life being frittered away by details, and he encourages us to simplify. Hmmm, good concept. Simplify! Seems like life becomes more and more complicated: five business checking accounts to manage, personal bank account, taxes, insurance, leases, cancellation policies, signs, newsletters, reviews, systems updating, schedules, bills, rent, mortgage, health care, generating and implementation of new ideas, team management, home care, pet care, etc.

I'm sure you can all relate! Whoa—we deal with a ton every day. I think there may be something to the whole simplify concept.

In the meantime, I may be making my life a bit more complicated with a showroom for TranquiliT {more to manage and larger expenses} while also opening up the Pink Palace for a real dining area which would simplify {I can entertain again, dine at my kitchen table, and peer out the windows currently covered by inventory}. It's all about balance! Yet another fine concept.

7. I HEART HOWARD SCHULTZ
March 2011

Today I was blessed with the opportunity to hear Starbucks's CEO, Howard Schultz, speak. I'm currently reading his first book, *Pour Your Heart Into It*, and squealed when a colleague told me he was speaking at George Washington University this week. I went on a mission to get tickets and showed up with bells on {plus sparkly legwarmers and hot pink rain boots = *tres* professional}.

I was star-struck and took lots of notes. I love humble beginnings fueled with passion—plus an ongoing effort to create a customer experience AND do-good {fair trade coffee beans, giving back to communities, health insurance for employees, etc.}. I purchased his latest book, *Onward: How Starbucks Fought for Its Life Without Losing Its Soul*, on my Kindle. Below are highlights and takeaways from his talk:

- Ensure an ongoing connection to values + guiding principles
- Love your business with every ounce of your soul {Amen!}
- Ask yourself what you are willing to sacrifice to achieve your dreams
- Dream big, then dream even bigger
- Get a strong education
- Surround yourself with people smarter than you
- Share your success with others
- Raise more equity than you think you need and sooner than you think you need
- Business is about each client interaction
- Early days were not really the "glory" days {Ah, I remember our church days}
- To grow, you must get your hands dirty and connect with biz roots
- When asked what type of coffee shop he would open today, he said he wouldn't—too much coffee. Would focus on a health and wellness store {yay Tranquil Space}
- Build intimate emotional connections with clients
- Build relationships + create a sense of community
- Two trends he's observing: less discretionary spending + more social media
- Must push for relevant innovation + preserve core purpose {ongoing at Tranquil Space!}

Never embrace mediocrity for profit

Go green: it's important to have employees happy to work for a company they believe in

When asked a question about work/life balance, he said it was a very personal decision to be discussed with one's partner. Must have alone time to recharge and time outside of the storm {when in crisis such as the 2008 economic downturn}. Needs support from family and friends. Can't do well unless healthy at home.

Rethink traditional marketing + PR

Ensure authentic, truthful, mindful communication with the world in non-marketing ways

To say the least, I was inspired and can't wait to finish his first book and dive into his second. I have professional crushes on so many: Zappos, lululemon, Starbucks, Apple, Patagonia, Martha Stewart, Danny Meyer {NYC restaurateur}. So many crushes, so little time.

How can you apply some of these ideas to your life and work? *Moi*: will continue to ponder, innovate, and seek ongoing authenticity to ensure everything I do is crafted with oodles of love.

8. ON MY MIND
July 2012

During my time at the World Domination Summit, I took heaps of notes—enjoyed sessions with inspiration powerhouses such Brene Brown, Scott Harrison {charity:water founder}, Danielle LaPorte, Scott Belsky, and Susannah Conway—and emerged feeling a bit, well, untapped.

What do I mean by untapped? That sinking feeling that your ship has sailed, other {younger} people are doing amazing things, and you're in a state of standstill. Nothing feels more uncomfortable to me than standing still. Clearly something I want and continue to work on. *Mindfulness, here I continue to come.*

This feeling began after hearing Scott's amazing story and thinking of my own big dreams for activist efforts. Sadly, the feeling continued through the entire summit. The summit ended with the summit founder, Chris Guillebeau, giving us each a $100 bill as we exited and challenging us to "start a project, surprise someone, or do something entirely different." Perfectly aligned with his awesome book, *$100 Startup*.

Even yesterday while chatting with a fellow participant at Susannah Conway's book event, it was clear that many of us were processing so much from the weekend. Ideas, inspiration, next steps, and ways to be. However, I haven't been able to quite shake that nagging feeling of being untapped. And I was frustrated with myself for not having an action plan yet. I mean, it had been nearly 24 hours since I left the summit! Hmmm, patience *is* a virtue.

It's the first time in awhile that I haven't been in the midst of launching something new or filled with a plan. Instead, I only have life planned through May 2013 when I finish social work school and am contemplating {insert drum roll} spending next summer in France writing and being. Ok, so that takes me through August 2013, then what?

After further reflection {and there is still lots of it to do}, I believe the untapped feeling comes with being in this odd state of "in between." In alignment with the summit's theme, I'm eager to live a remarkable life in a conventional world and am questioning the how. How do I take all the weekend notes and infuse them into my daily life? How do I live a remarkable life in a conventional world? How do I live more mindfully? How do I know I'm doing enough? How do I make a difference for the animals? How do I on and on and on.

Ever have these feelings and moments of questioning? Having devoted the past 13 years to the birth and growth of my baby, Tranquil Space, plus various offspring {TranquiliT, *Tranquility du Jour*, Tranquil Space Foundation}, I'm slowly transitioning. To what? I don't know. Definitely don't plan to send my babies off to college as I'm too attached. Yet I have this longing to connect, sink deeper within, and slow down. Time will tell. In the interim, I need to battle my own untapped feelings and remember that I am enough. We are enough. You are enough.

While standing in the journal section of Powell's last night, I smiled in honor of the dreams, hopes, and fears that will soon be penned into these beautiful beings. Now, take a moment and answer this question: how will you live a remarkable life in a conventional world? Here are my off the cuff thoughts:

- Simplify
- Seek beauty
- Give freely
- Sprinkle sunshine
- Bask in being different
- Embrace change
- Leave a small eco footprint
- Leave a big "heartprint" {*oui*, I made that word up—a bad habit}

Et toi? It's a big question worthy of big journaling. Oh, and another gentle reminder. You. Are. Enough.

9. ADVENTURES IN TRANQUILIT
November 2012

Launched in 2002 with yoga pants and tees {that's where the name TranquiliT{ee} came from}, I dreamed of a cozy clothing line that aligned with an active lifestyle—quickly moving from yoga class to bookstore browsing to café dates.

A lover of style since my early days hiking Oklahoma hills donning a bonnet with purse in tow, I fell in love with Units and Multiples {mix and match clothing} in my teen years.

In 2004 I took the yoga pants and tees a step further by adding trendy tunics and dresses—flowy, flattering designs to fit many bodies—to wear alone or over yoga pants, as well as armwarmers, legwarmers, and luxurious wraps.

At Greenfestival this year, I shared the 10-year journey of TranquiliT to a small audience. One suggested resource I mention is *The Fashion Designer Survival Guide* by Mary Gehlhar. I'm most proud of having the line locally sewn, planting 150 trees each month to help offset carbon emissions, and donating a portion of proceeds to amazing charities doing good work for women and the earth. Seeing women don the line for weddings, yoga, travel, and beyond always brings a smile to my face. I'm honored to be a small catalyst in helping women feel comfy and chic at the same time. Peruse our latest collection's look book at TranquiliT.com for a sprinkle of inspiration.

What beckons you to bring it into existence?

10. THE NAME TRANQUIL SPACE
June 2014

I'm fresh back from a week in the tropics with co-host Mary Catherine Starr and a beautiful group of yogis. We ate lots of fresh fruit, practiced hours of yoga, sipped water from coconuts, explored creative endeavors such as mixed media and writing, and aligned our sleep with the sun. It's always an honor to hit the reset button.

As we move closer to the celebration of our 15th year, I'm continuing the storytelling of our humble beginnings: this piece is about how the name Tranquil Space came to be and why it matters.

On a 4th floor walk-up at 16th and U, Yoga at Kimberly's began to welcome yogis from across the city and as far as McLean, Virginia and Bowie, Maryland. Some saw the flier at a local business, others saw the mention in the classifieds of *City Paper* under "instruction," and a few were personal friends. Either way, they all gathered in search of tranquility. An oasis in a transient, fast-paced, demanding city.

As we began the transition from my walk-up to a church parlor, I wanted to replace Yoga at Kimberly's with something that evoked emotion, served as a respite, and beckoned the soul to rest. While sitting around a living room with fellow Women's Business Center colleagues, Tranquil Space was coined. And it stuck. And it's offered me a gentle reminder many times a day of what matters most. Tranquility.

Among the eight limbs of yoga, *pratayahara* is encouraged. It means withdrawal of the senses. The ability to be in the midst of chaos and find stillness. Most people can find tranquility on a secluded beach, at a silent meditation retreat, or in a favorite yoga class. But finding tranquility among deadlines, a chilling diagnosis, or the end of a relationship is challenging. The fifth limb of yoga encourages steadiness at all times. That's a tranquil space within.

> Finding tranquility among deadlines, a chilling diagnosis, or the end of a relationship is challenging. The fifth limb of yoga encourages steadiness at all times.

While penning the Mindful Monday muse yesterday, I used the Viktor Frankl quote: "Between stimulus and response there is a space. In that space is our power to choose. In our response lies our growth and our freedom." Despite the fact that I've read it, resonated with it, and shared it for years, the use of "space" within the quote seemed perfect for the description of our 15-year-old community.

The studio offers us the opportunity to practice. To practice being with discomfort {hello arm balances}. To practice self-compassion. To practice being in our bodies. And, ideally, the space to choose our response to the stimuli of daily life. In that response lies our growth and our freedom from patterns that no longer serve us. Choose with compassion.

May you bask in that space of tranquility. Thus, Tranquil Space. *Namaste.*

ENTREPRENEURSHIP NUGGETS

1. It often takes years to see the fruits of your labor.
2. Ensure an ongoing connection to your values.
3. Build relationships and a sense of community.

~ ENTREPRENEURSHIP TAKEAWAYS ~

CHAPTER 7: Activism

How wonderful it is that nobody need wait a single moment before starting to improve the world. —Anne Frank

One sunny Friday afternoon, I stood outside the National Press Building in Washington, D.C. holding a sign protesting Walmart's treatment of pigs while their executives were inside discussing their environmental initiatives. While many businesses have begun to phase out inhumane gestation crates where female pigs are confined to a two-foot by six-foot stall unable to turn around, Walmart has not followed suit. My mother was in town so she joined me, along with a fellow pig-loving friend, Carol. As people passed by, a fellow protester distributed an informative flier and recipients seemed engaged. A group of school children walked past on an outing and one asked, "Why are the pigs in jail?" Great question, little one. Why *are* they in jail?

The posts in this chapter include tips on being a spiritual activist, organizations I've enjoyed supporting over the years, why I returned to school to pursue a social work degree, an outline of creating a charity event, the importance of listening to your soul, my deep love of animals, and more.

Dictionary.com defines activism as "the doctrine or practice of vigorous action or involvement as a means of achieving political or other goals, sometimes by demonstrations, protests, etc." And I believe it can be expressed in many ways—from the way we spend our money, time, energy, and overall daily efforts. Each decision is an opportunity to do more good and less harm.

Tune into Tranquility du Jour podcasts #256, #301, #318 for more insights on activism.

1. PLANTING SEEDS
July 2006

Last night was our first official Tranquil Space Foundation planning session. We discussed ideas ranging from yoga in prisons to a "breathe in" to empowering teen girls. With a vision as broad as creating a tranquil space in our society, it is hard to determine our signature event in addition to our current charity community. The more I mull it over, the more I lean toward work with teenage girls.

> Being an activist is the rent we pay for being on the planet.
> —Alice Walker

Can you imagine the power of meeting mentors during those awkward formative years who remind you that you can be anything you dream, that you possess a ton of potential {as we all do}, and teach you to work with your body rather than fight against it? Wow, now that could have the potential to make a profound effect on blooming women! So many options and I'm delighted to watch the vision unfold for our new non-profit.

tranquilspacefoundation.org

2. SPIRITUAL ACTIVISM
May 2007

I'm still adjusting to my "normal" routine, as it's been less than two weeks since I returned to D.C. after my Jivamukti teacher training intensive. Whew! As I write this from a hotel room near Chicago {here for a yoga conference}, I wanted to summarize percolating thoughts on carrying yoga off the mat through spiritual activism.

Activism is an intentional act to bring about social change. If we incorporate spirituality, we're bringing about social change for something greater than oneself. I love exploring ways to be a spiritual activist in daily life and have put together some of my favorites.

Give graciously: Consider alternative gifts to the standard new set of slippers. This year my mother got a goat for the holidays. The goat was purchased to provide milk for a family in Africa. Yep, a goat. If you own a business or manage a team, encourage your staff to volunteer and compensate them for their time doing so.

Volunteer: The good vibes associated with volunteering are contagious. Give of your time and energy. The yogic teaching of greedlessness {*aparigraha*} is embodied when we give freely of our time, resources, and goodwill. Help somebody who looks like they need assistance.

Veg out: By choosing a vegetarian diet, you can reduce the suffering of other beings and create a sustainable environment in which all can thrive. And as liberal foodie intellectual Michael Pollan encourages, "Eat food. Not too much. Mostly plants."

Be a good citizen: Share your voice and vote. Stay abreast of what is happening around you. Do your share to contribute to your community. If you have a small patch of grass in front of your city condo, plant pansies or an English boxwood. Pick up trash when you walk past it on the street. See local plays. Shop at farmers' markets and from indie designers.

Fill a need: Does your office recycle? Gather the information on how to get started and request a meeting with the decision-maker to present the data. When you see something missing in your community, why not get the ball rolling as the pioneer of the moment? Let your actions leave a legacy.

Practice mindfulness: Start each day by lighting a candle, sitting in meditation, and setting an intention for the day. Listen when people talk to you. Chew your food. End each day with reflection. Interact with others in a respectful and reverent way.

Go green: Recycle and reduce your household waste by becoming mindful of the resources you consume. According to Patanjali, author of the *Yoga Sutras*, we are to cultivate a "steady and joyful connection to the earth" so let's take steps to reduce our carbon footprint. Support eco-friendly products. Take a stand. Plant a tree.

Live by example: Be a source of inspiration to others. Let your life be a story that will affect others for years to come. Smile at people as you walk by them. Say "thank you." Ask your colleague how she is and mean it.

Being a spiritual activist is a state of mind. Practice it in all situations. Spiritual activism

~ READER FEEDBACK ~

On a bone china platter, encircled by pink petals

Tranquility du Jour, la pièce de résistance...

or not.

No, not resistance,

surrender.

Welcoming, cozy, mindful,

attending to creation of a new realm.

Sounding the slippery shifting paradigms

of relaxed innovation.

Rewiring synapses, fine-tuning the mind,

blazing new paths into the known,

the unknown and the may-never-be-known...

but only experienced.

Serve it forth!

Maite, France
villaparisienne.blogspot.fr

is a way of life and you offer a unique footprint. Do you have visions of joining the Peace Corps or helping build homes in Haiti? Or is your vision focused more on nurturing a family or planting a small community garden space in the city?

Whatever it is, personalize it, ensure it reflects your values, and take action. View your resources as powerful forces for doing good and making a difference. Incorporate this notion every time you step onto the mat by dedicating your yoga practice as a way to serve the world. Recognize the interconnectedness of all beings. Our actions have a global impact. Time and money are valuable commodities. Choose wisely. *Namaste*.

3. LET'S GIVE BACK
January 2010

Wondering how to make a difference? Questioning your legacy? I wanted to share my end of year giving plans. There are numerous ways to give back and do good. A few simple everyday ideas are saying "thank you," sending a thinking of you note, giving a homemade gift, volunteering your time, donating money, or even simply spreading word about a good cause/event online or via word of mouth. In *Tranquilista* I outline how to host a ChariTea soirée to help raise awareness of a special cause.

My first activist efforts began with tithing my $2 weekly allowance at church. Then I became obsessed with turtles. Raised my own and donated my allowance to "the turtle lady" in South Padre Island. We even took Myrtle to the vet when she got ill {thanks Mom and Dad} and held Christmas parties for them {whole *other* blog post}. Ah, grade school enthusiasm was the launch of my do-gooding efforts!

Giving always feels so good. This year I chose to donate to:

Mid-Atlantic Pug Rescue—Yay for adopting animals. Confession: since I'm losing on my battle to mother a potbelly pig, I'd LOVE to adopt a pug from this fabulous organization.

Trees for the Future—Sponsored another grove of trees thanks to all class passes and massages purchased at Tranquil Space. GREAT gift idea!

Friends of the Animals—Amazing organization doing phenomenal work. I receive their great magazine *Actionline* and focused my donation primarily on primates. I heart monkeys.

Tranquil Space Foundation—As co-founder of this organization, the mission is incredibly close to my heart. We give microgrants and bring yoga, creativity, and leadership to women and girls through our Tranquil Teens program.

My Sister's Place—When we began selling Tranquil Space tees I wanted to find an organization for donating a portion of sales. As a women's studies grad student at the time, I chose My Sister's Place, which works to eradicate domestic violence. One in four women report experiencing domestic violence in their lifetime.

Washington Humane Society—Half of all our beverage sales at Tranquil Space are donated here. I *adore* this organization and look forward to their annual Sugar + Champagne event, hosting our annual Doga class, and monthly adoption events outside our bustling 17th Street location.

Greenpeace—A few years ago I came upon one of their workers at Dupont Circle on a very cold day. She showed me images of the polar bears on melting glaciers and I signed up for monthly donations. Yes, I'm an easy target.

ASPCA—If you watch the commercial with Sarah Mclachlan, you'll donate, too! I have a monthly donation set up to this organization that does amazing work for the animals.

Farm Sanctuary—Tranquil Space adopted JD {a big pig} and Travolta {a big cow}. Le Beau and I visited them in 2008. See videos of our visit at YouTube.com/tranqulitydujour.

Red Apes—I've always had a fascination with orangutans and Tranquil Space adopted Dodo this year. Cutest ape ever!

There are SO many deserving organizations and causes out there. I hope this post gives some ideas on various ways to become an activist. What are your favorite organizations? How do you give back through small gestures, donations, volunteering, or compassion?

Here's to being a do-gooder this year and beyond!

4. IF I RULED THE WORLD
August 2010

Hello from a Starbucks in Austin, Texas. Le Beau and I spent the weekend with my aunt and uncle in hill country sipping vino, sitting in the creek, checking in constantly on Le Pug at camp parents, and answering oodles of emails back home. In addition we got to spend time with a dear family who I've known since birth. Always nice to have people in your life whom have

known you for so long. They brought photos of me donning preppy Cole Haan shoes, khaki skirt, and chambray shirt with a huge blond perm, and overly tall bangs. Those *were* the days. Thank gawd they're gone!

I have been pondering a fun blog post titled "If I ruled the world." Here are a few ideas for it:

- The smell of lavender would be everywhere
- There would be no obesity {BIG problem here in Texas} or ill health
- Cows, pigs, chicken, turkeys, duck, turtles—everything would roam free
- Neighbors would know {and like} each other
- We would all practice mindful communication
- There would be no poverty
- Political parties would have compassion for each others' views
- We would spend as much time exercising as watching TV
- Women's studies and social work would be required classes in university
- So would traveling and studying abroad
- Education would be required and free {not sure who pays for it but hey, I'm dreaming BIG}
- There would be no animal abuse or exploitation of any kind
- Eco-fashion would be the norm
- Fast food would be organic, fresh, and local
- Soda fountains would distribute fair trade teas, not Coke
- Women would hold numerous positions of power—as many, if not more, than men
- Mid-day naps and meditation would be a must in law firms, corporations, non-profits, schools, and more!

Ok, a few far-fetched ideas, but they felt good writing. What if *you* ruled the world?

Off to an Austin book signing!

5. WHY SOCIAL WORK?
March 2012

I'm often asked what I plan to do with my master's in social work {MSW} and why I'm pursuing it. I've pondered a blog post about it for months and decided it would be perfect for today's Tranquilosophy piece. For longtime readers, you may recall my "I'm returning to grad school" announcement May 2009 from Costa Rica. Poor Le Beau read it on my blog before seeing my email to him.

It was a big decision as I pondered the next decade post-Tranquil Space turning 10. Grad school's been a long journey of juggling businesses, health, relationships, and transitions but I'm on the homestretch {one year and one month to go}. And it feels good.

Social work will offer the education and experience to continue planting more and more seeds. Here are the three ways I plan to use my MSW:

1. Continued growth and development of our non-profit, Tranquil Space Foundation.

2. Working 1:1 with clients on a deeper level than I can currently offer through mentoring.

3. Social justice and activism for animals, particularly farm animals.

Where does that leave yoga, eco-fashion, a blog and a podcast? Exactly where it is! These are all part of my DNA, big passions, and sweet babies. As I look to grow and do my best to leave an inspirational legacy, I see my MSW as expanding my tranquility toolkit. If all goes as planned, I graduate May 2013 and look forward to continuing to incorporate all I'm learning into my various roles.

> Social work will offer the education and experience to continue planting more and more seeds.

6. MY LIFE IS MY MESSAGE
August 2012

Last night I was reading *Most Good, Least Harm: A Simple Principle for a Better World and Meaningful Life* by Zoe Weil before falling asleep. I recently signed up for an online course through her Institute for Humane Education, and this is our course book. I love it so far and came across this great piece in her book titled "model your message and work for change." A light bulb went off.

I've been reveling in a compliment and this beautiful teaching aligns perfectly. While hosting the second Paris + Provence retreat this summer, a longtime reader of *Tranquility du Jour* said, "You're just like you are online."

Although it was an off-the-cuff remark, it was just what I needed to hear. It felt like validation that my life was indeed my message and the two were in sync {at least in France}. It felt good.

When reading, "To create a peaceful world, we must each make our lives mirrors of the world we want" and that Gandhi answered a reporter with "my life is my message," I was excited to pen this post.

It's important to note that sometimes we fall short. As I've shared, after I got my fave yoga mantra, *Lokah Samastah Sukhino Bhavantu*, tattooed on my arm, but found myself getting snippy with a not-so-pleasant postal employee, I took a deep breath and remembered my message. It was kindness, not reactive aggression. Le sigh.

Weil goes on to state:

Modeling our message—walking the talk—may be the most challenging task before each of us. It is, in my mind, a spiritual discipline that is as demanding and difficult as any practice could ever be. It begins with being kind, respectful, and honest in your interactions, but it doesn't end there. Modeling your message also entails making choices about products, clothing, transportation, recreation, food, volunteerism, and work that reflect your values and are peaceful, humane, restorative, and sustainable.

If you were to sum up your message in a sentence or two, what would it say? Remember, we're not seeking perfection. It's an impossible challenge. We're human. We make mistakes. We react. We get our buttons pushed. We feel emotions we don't understand. However, as the Dalai Lama reminds us, "Be kind whenever possible. It is always possible." May this be a part of our message.

7. 15 MONTHS OF EFFORT
September 2012

Last night was the long anticipated *fête* I was asked to host for Pigs Animal Sanctuary in July 2011. Naturally I was over the moon {I mean, *anything* for my beloved sponsored pig Walter} to make the festivities happen and here's an idea of what goes into an event like this:

One year out
- Set date
- Secure speaker
- Secure venue
- Had 20th anniversary + I heart Pigs logo created
- Secure entertainment {we had a piano player}

4 months out
- Creation of promo postcards
- Secure speaker lodging and travel

2 months out
- Set up Facebook invite
- Secure guest gift {we had pink lavender-scented locally-made soaps in the shape of pigs}
- Secure volunteers {greeters, sales, floaters, etc.}
- Reach out to many amazing individuals for silent auction donations
- Secure photographer

2 weeks out
- Set up online silent auction and promote heavily online

- Use pig stamp + pen "thank you" on tags for tying around guest gifts
- Order flowers for the event

Ongoing
- Promotion via social media
- Distribution of promo postcards
- Coordinate with speaker
- Communication with board

Day of
- Create ambiance {flowers, music, signs}
- Set up square + paper system for credit card processing
- Volunteer orientation
- Create in person silent auction signs and bid sheets
- Prep and finalize speech
- Haul heaps of items to event {books, tees, signs, gifts, auction items, flowers, vases}
- Finalize bill with venue
- Play hostess

After event
- Heaps of bookkeeping: tally up ticket sales, product sales, in person and online auction sales
- Mail online auction wins
- Write and mail thank yous to silent auction donors
- Update board of directors on event
- Distribute photos
- Pay final bills

Whew! This was one of my biggest events to do solo, and if it wasn't for the lovely Marie Champagne {*bonjour* best last name ever}, it couldn't have happened. This morning I feel blessed, exhausted, and so very honored for the 40ish people who showed last night to support Pigs and to the many {including Mama Wilson} who bid on the great online auction items.

Merci for assisting *moi* on this journey of causing less suffering and more compassion.

8. INTERCONNECTEDNESS
March 2013

Wednesday was a typical day at internship. Lots of clients, projects, phone calls, and our second hosting of a company-wide well-being webinar. Oh, and a fun dinner party to host at *chez moi* that evening!

This all changed while crossing the tracks en route to the station for lunch. My fellow intern and I passed a pigeon that didn't fly away as we got closer. I knelt down and saw the pigeon wasn't doing well. We got concerned and I held him gently while petting his sweet feathery round body. My colleague chased down nearby track workers asking them to help noting, "my colleague is very upset." So two burly men rode up on their carts to offer assistance.

Then I got nervous about them helping as I didn't know what they could do, so I said we'd transport him to a safer location than the train tracks. His neck appeared to be broken, he couldn't fly, but he could walk and would often come upright from time to time. We lovingly placed him in another area and went to the station somewhat traumatized. My colleague noted, "now he has more dignity." That stuck with me. What a social worky thing to say!

When we returned, he'd moved a few feet and was upright and seemed to be doing a bit better. However, I couldn't shake it. Headed back to my desk and Googled, "what do pigeons eat" and "how to care for a pigeon with a broken neck." The websites recommended calling a vet for help. I found the nearby vet, called them, and was referred to the Washington Humane Society. Called them and was referred to Animal Control. Called them and they dispatched an officer. I took a deep breath.

I headed out to check on him again and he'd moved a bit further, but still looked sad.

Back inside I went to get a box and asked if I could bring him inside until the officer arrived. My supervisor offered a box, but wasn't keen on a pigeon in the office. *C'est la vie.* Took the box out, got him situated, and added a brick inside so it wouldn't blow away. Ahhhh, then I became concerned that the train station police may get nervous about an empty box on the side of their building. Ran back inside, got a Sharpie, and penned "injured pigeon. Animal control coming, please do not move" onto the box.

En route back to the office to assist with webinar set up, I passed an officer and squealed, "Are you with Animal Control?" Apparently he'd been looking for the pigeon but wasn't given my cell number from the dispatcher. He couldn't have been sweeter. He toted the injured pigeon to safety after gently wrapping him in a tiny blanket. He said it looked like the pigeon may have a virus causing neck issues and he'd take it back to give it fluids and assess. Ah, success! D.C. Animal Control is 202.576.6664 and now highlighted in my contacts.

Sure, in the grand scheme of things, this act is minor. However, I like to think it made a big difference to this one feathery friend. What small choices do you make each day that can enhance or detract from the quality of your life or someone whose life you share? Yep, even a little pigeon. We truly *are* interconnected.

~ Reader Feedback ~

I found Kimberly's podcast and, shortly afterwards, her blog in 2008, the year I finished a relationship, sold my house, and moved to Spain more full-time. It was a time of great upheaval for me and yet I found some grounding. *Tranquility du Jour* was a kind of healing not just for the changes in my life at that moment but for the changes I wanted to make longer term.

Since listening to that first podcast, I felt something of a kindred spirit in Kimberly. Something in her joy and curiosity about life, something about her struggles and the way that she chooses to deal with them. The fact that she has an idea to do something and she tries it. In so many ways she inspires me, in other ways she assures me that it is ok to be like that. She is completely different to me and yet some things are essentially the same. I feel that I can say that only because she always writes so honestly about things that matter to us as humans. Her mixture of travel, yoga, activism, creativity, business, and psychology could be quite an intense lot but instead she makes it fun and light by sprinkling and infusing everything with sparkle and shine. Each podcast and every blog post is thought provoking in some way or another not only because of the constant reminder to seek tranquility but because she constantly inspires us to look into things a little deeper, think a little differently while following our own hearts.

I felt angry for a long time about so many things in life that I felt were unjust or plain wrong. I felt angry and powerless to do anything. I did activist things such as participating in demonstrations, reading and engaging in local politics and environmental groups. I believe that the biggest impact that *Tranquility du Jour* {and the many signposts that it offers} has had in my life has been to realize, and constantly realize, that the best activist I can be is the one who lives well and has inner tranquility which can be passed on to friends and strangers alike. Where our actions and attitudes, by being present and changing small things locally, can actually create communities {as Kimberly demonstrates in her many businesses and non profit involvements} which, in our day and age, can like a stone thrown into a calm pool of water, send ripples and reverberations around our planet affecting many more communities. I am very grateful for being able to read *Tranquility du Jour* and being, for the most part, a silent member of its community. Thank you Kimberly!

Catherine Emily Pickard, England, living in Spain
classroomcat.blogspot.com

9. MINDFUL EATING
October 2013

Farm Sanctuary is one of the beneficiaries of Tranquility Tour. We had a lovely Meetup in New York and got to see the sanctuary near Los Angeles today. And to top it off, we happened to be in town for the Los Angeles Walk for Farm Animals which made me *very* happy considering I had to sign up as a Sleep in for Farm Animals D.C. participant this year since we're on the road.

Curious? Learn more about the environmental destruction of factory farming. Consider adopting a farm animal. Join Farm Sanctuary's compassionate communities. Be an advocate. Find good recipes on websites such as goveg.com. Promote veg eating. Try Meatless Mondays. Stay stocked with veg snacks like fruit and veggies, raw almonds, soy yogurt, hummus, blue corn chips, and salsa. Try meat substitutes like MorningStar. Start by phasing out red meat, then white meat. Take a B12 supplement and multivitamin. Limit added sugar intake and watch the documentary *Fed Up* for inspiration. Befriend quinoa, tempeh, beans, and nuts. According to the website Counting Animals, a vegetarian saves 34 land animals, 219 fish, and 151 shellfish each year which comes to 404 animals! Enjoy feeling lighter. Check out an animal sanctuary near you. Explore compassionate food choices.

Yoga teacher Sharon Gannon reminds us, "Through the practices of yoga, we discover that concern for the happiness and well being of others, including animals, must be an essential part of our own quest for happiness and well being. The fork can be a powerful weapon of mass destruction or a tool to create peace on earth."

Our health, the environment, and the animals deserve better.

> The fork can be a powerful weapon of mass destruction or a tool to create peace on earth.
> —Sharon Gannon

10. HEART ANIMALS
March 2014

While in NYC yesterday I met with Richard Zimmerman of Orangutan Outreach and my deep passion for animals was touched. I noticed myself drawn to his stories, eager to find ways to help the furry orange creatures, and tearing up as we spoke about the atrocities against them due to the palm oil crisis {the palm oil industry, which is causing clear-cutting of forests, is one of the most important factors for the dramatic reduction of orangutan populations}. He even showed me his tattoo of Luna, one of my first adoptees who went missing mysteriously.

As I left our time together at Stumptown Coffee en route to my memoir writing class I was full of a special kind of energy. Something I hadn't felt so strongly possibly since Farm Sanctuary's End Factory Farming Conference of 2011. While hastily sprinting to writing class, I texted Le Beau that we needed to drop everything and head to Borneo. The orangutans needed us.

My deep connection to animals traces back to grade school. There were the many carelessly abandoned cats and dogs that became our family's beloved pets. Followed by numerous fish, newts, and hamsters. But it was turtles that became my first true obsession. Starting with a red-eared baby named Myrtle, I built a small village culminating in a holiday celebration complete with a Christmas tree, carols, and freeze-dried worm stocking stuffers for her and her rescued siblings.

I even told turtle stories for all my third grade writing projects until Mrs. Stever {you see I've let this go} told me I need to come up with a new topic. Apparently she, and possibly my classmates, had tired of my turtle tales. The obsession continued with an extensive collec-

tion of turtle figurines in pewter, stone, and plaster, but no more stories. Or live turtles. They'd all gone to turtle heaven despite vet visits, numerous reptile books, and lots of love. And, yes, they were buried in our backyard.

My next obsession was apes, particularly orangutans although I was also a fan of chimps and gorillas. After watching *Gorillas in the Mist* as a young girl, I've idolized women who devote their lives and souls to a cause, especially animals. In college I was gifted an annual zoo pass to feed my ape-visiting {some would say stalking} addiction. I was particularly fond of the baby orangutan Mango. I'd drag my poor boyfriend up for regular visits, snap heaps of photos with the glare of the glass caught by the flash, and head back to the sorority house revitalized. As if I'd connected to a real world, something very different than my sorority existence.

Pre-Internet, I sent away for info on gorilla treks in Africa and began saving to meet these giants. Then I moved to D.C., started a business, and my funds and energy went elsewhere. But I haven't forgotten the gorillas, Dian Fossey, or the way my heart pounds as I get close to the ape house at zoos. {Although I'm not a fan of animals in captivity, I am grateful for the opportunity to see these lovely beings up close}.

Next came exposure to Farm Sanctuary during the 2007 Jivamukti month-long teacher training. That's when I adopted couch-sized JD and have been pig-obsessed ever since. From hosting fundraising and awareness-raising events, to adopting pigs, to hosting film screenings, to feeding them heaps of animal crackers, to craving one of my own. My soul desires all beings be free from suffering. Especially the beautiful pigs.

My favorite mantra means, "May all beings everywhere be happy and free. May the thoughts, words, and actions of my own life contribute in some way to that happiness and to that freedom for all." This translation of *Lokah Samastah Sukhino Bhavantu* by yoga teacher Sharon Gannon emphasizes how our thoughts, words, and actions have an impact on others, all beings. We are given the opportunity to choose kindness with each meal, purchase, communication, and beyond.

Today is Meatout day. A day dedicated to compassionate eating. As you consider your breakfast, lunch, dinner, and savory snacks, I encourage you to choose veg. It's fairly easy, most tasty, less expensive, and healthier. And no animals harmed. A win-win.

As I continue to find my way as a cheerleader for animal rights, I know it's where I belong. The emotion that bubbles up when I'm around creatures is palpable. It's like I'm home. I come alive and I want to give up everything I have to immerse myself in the cause. Then reality hits. A mortgage is due. There are yogis to be served. And I have a big beautiful family that I love.

However, if you see an out-of-office love note posted on the blog declaring I've run away to Borneo, you'll know why. Pigs and orangutans make me swoon. Sponsor one of your own. Forgo products with palm oil or pork. Let your passionate freak flag fly whether it is for turtles, cats, human rights, or the environment. I'll be right there with you waving my own.

> May all beings everywhere be happy and free. May the thoughts, words, and actions of my own life contribute in some way to that happiness and to that freedom for all.

ACTIVISM NUGGETS

1. Practice intentional acts to bring social change.

2. Observe your interconnectedness to all beings.

3. Make your life your message.

~ ACTIVISM TAKEAWAYS ~

A FAVORITE POST-CLASS READING AT TRANQUIL SPACE:

There is a story of a woman running away from tigers. She runs and runs, and the tigers are getting closer and closer. When she comes to the edge of a cliff, she sees some vines there, so she climbs down and holds on to the vines.

Looking down, she sees that there are tigers below her as well. She then notices that a mouse is gnawing away at the vine to which she is clinging. She also sees a beautiful little bunch of strawberries close to her, growing out of a clump of grass. She looks up and she looks down. She looks at the mouse. Then she just takes a strawberry, puts it in her mouth, and enjoys it thoroughly.

Tigers above, tigers below. This is actually the predicament that we are always in, in terms of our birth and death. Each moment is just what it is. It might be the only moment of our life, it might be the only strawberry we'll ever eat. We could get depressed about it, or we could finally appreciate it and delight in the preciousness of every single moment of our life.

From *The Wisdom of No Escape and the Path of Loving-Kindness* by Pema Chödrön

CHAPTER 8:
Mindfulness

*The best way to capture moments is to pay attention.
This is how we cultivate mindfulness. Mindfulness means being awake.
It means knowing what you are doing.* —Jon Kabat-Zinn

While putting one foot in front of the other and intentionally during a mindfulness-based stress reduction {MBSR} training with Jon Kabat-Zinn, I found my chest heating with frustration. It was the fifth time I'd heard, "now walking meditation," that day. I mean, how much more of this could I take? As I looked out on the other 200 participants lifting, shifting, and slowly placing their feet, a sense of hilarity eased the discomfort. We looked like zombies. Then my gaze moved to the flat concrete slab where Jon was walking with ease and focus. My body softened and I returned to the practice. He made walking meditation seem like the most important thing in the world at that moment. And indeed it was.

When contemplating tranquility {a daily occurrence}, I continually return to mindfulness as the key to tasting it. As defined by Jon, mindfulness is "the awareness that emerges through paying attention on purpose, in the present moment, and nonjudgmentally to the unfolding of experience moment by moment." Through the pieces chosen for this chapter, you'll find takeaways from my first introduction to MBSR, a not-so-big life workshop, the trouble with perfection, busyness, and the importance of taking a pause.

Tune into Tranquility du Jour *podcasts #120, #267, #321
for more insights on mindfulness.*

1. MINDFULNESS-BASED STRESS REDUCTION
October 2009

> Change is the essence of life. Be willing to surrender what you are for what you could become.
> —author unknown

This past weekend I was blessed with the opportunity to bask in three hours of discussion and practice of mindfulness-based stress reduction with the talented surgeon-cum-mindfulness-teacher Gina Sager. Her words of wisdom have haunted me, in a good way, since Sunday. As a very-*vata*-need-some-grounding-doer, I was struck by her simple, yet powerful statements. I kept raising my hand and asking, "Ok, great tips but how do I practice it *now* . . . and for how long and how often?" I love prescriptions, five simple steps, or a book that will bring the topic to life and help me embody it *now*. Unfortunately, this practice is all about, well, practice.

In our fast-paced society we love quick fixes. Yoga and meditation offer impressive results but we have to make the time to practice. Ah, work. Practice may have a negative connotation, especially if it reminds you of swimming or ballet lessons when your teacher encouraged you to practice, practice, practice. I'd like us to reframe it in a positive light—as an opportunity. Ultimately an opportunity to let go. Surrender. Embrace change.

Here are my takeaways from the beautiful Sunday morning session in our Bamboo studio:

1. Do this work to benefit those who share your life—a beautiful reminder of our interconnectedness.

2. It matters what you do and *how* you do it.

3. Mindfulness is moment-to-moment nonjudgmental awareness.

4. Obstacles are our teachers. Become comfortable with discomfort.

5. Taking time to create space between thought and action allows us to transform how we react.

6. Everything you do and think matters because it affects others.

7. We sit in meditation to train the mind to become more conscious.

8. Balance effort and surrender.

9. Focus on the exhale = let go.

10. It takes 20 minutes for the mind to settle down.

Wow, sounds so simple, right? Such profound, challenging work. Sit still. Be. Breathe. Quiet thoughts. Explore this beautiful complement to doing. Start your day with a few minutes of seated meditation. Take a mid-day break to savor a walking meditation around your office building. End your day with ten minutes of reflection. By taking time to nurture yourself, you are able to be fully present and compassionate toward others. Take five deep breaths and let go.

2. SURGERY MUSINGS
April 2010

Life is full of lessons. Some welcomed. Some not-so-welcomed. I've been "blessed" with an interesting one of my own this past week: shoulder surgery. In December 2008 I began having a tweak in my shoulder, but carried on assuming it would pass. Finally, growing frustrated, I headed to an orthopedist last summer, began physical therapy, and even got a cortisone injection. Ouch! Still in pain, I returned this year for an MRI, and they found a bone spur that would require surgery. Got it scheduled and was wheeled in donning blue scrub attire last Thursday.

My normal *modus operandi* has been turned upside down. Of course when I got home from surgery I was still numb, so I whipped out my laptop, carried flowers, candles, and incense into the bedroom, and fell into my old patterns. As the numbness wore off, I was a mess. Couldn't move, get comfortable, eat, or email. My excitement over being able to rest for a few days was slowly wearing off and reality was setting in. This surgery *was* a big deal. Not only did he remove the bone spur, but he found the dreaded rotator cuff tear that means months of healing versus weeks. Uh oh, looks like I'll be *sans chaturanga* for awhile.

This past week has been full of lessons and it felt apropos to share these in my April muse. Patterns are hard to break. Pema Chödrön sums this up beautifully in *Wisdom of No Escape,* where she writes that the same old demons {lessons} will continue to show up until we learn the lessons they came to teach us. Hmmmm.

> No matter how cold the winter, spring is sure to follow.
> —Proverb

Over the past decade I've become addicted to rushing from meeting to meeting, being accessible via email at all times, overscheduling, wanting a quick fix {I'm the one in meditation workshops asking, "so what is the perfect formula?"}, and juggling multiple projects and deadlines at once. Is this surgery going to stop this addiction? I don't know the answer to that one, but it has forced me to slow down substantially. For most of this week I've been handling emails, shipping online TranquiliT orders, and doing day-to-day tasks with my non-dominant hand. Clearly, that slows down the process substantially.

I've been savoring the *most* phenomenal book over the past month called *The Not So Big Life*, and I can't recommend it highly enough. The premise of the book is to slow down, savor, single-task, and still get things down. Written from a Zen perspective, it is the perfect off-the-yoga-mat book. This book and my surgery are sure to instill some change.

As spring blossoms around us, I, too, hope to bloom in a new way. Due to my MSW class schedule, my teaching schedule will shift this summer into the following year. I've held tight to my classes, even teaching on my birthday or getting back in town early to teach. Life has a way of shaking things up so we don't get comfortable. This change—along with my forced slowing down, healing and recovery process, and dedication to living this not-so-big life—is destined to have an impact. I look forward to sharing the journey with you.

May this new month and fresh season offer you, too, a chance to reflect on patterns that feel out of sync. How can you bring more mindfulness into your every day? What is calling for attention deep within? Listen intently. Or it may come forth without a pretty bow tied around it {ex. forced slowing down due to surgery}.

Life is full of lessons and discoveries. If only we'll listen. Sip tea. Take a walk. Do legs up the wall. Write in your journal. Bask in being. Your soul will thank you.

3. NOT SO BIG LIFE
December 2010

When I saw that Sarah Susanka was going to be at Kripalu mid-December, I knew I must sign up. What a divine way to end 2010—participating in a year-end review with an author whose book was instrumental to mine. It was fortuitous to start the decade at Kripalu in 2000 and to end it there as well. Such a blessing.

Friday began at 5:00 a.m. with a train ride to New York. The train to Kripalu travels along the Hudson River for two hours. Ahhhhh. Arrived to a snowscape of tranquility. Played catch up in the café with my laptop for a few hours, noshed on yummy food, and headed to my first session all about intros for the 26 participants. A beautiful blend of women and two men. My excitement kept me up, and I didn't sleep well.

Up early for morning meditation and an eight-hour day of workshops, greeted by a dreamy sunrise. Sarah encouraged us to see thoughts as champagne bubbles. Oh, how I loved that imagery. The time together was oodles of processing and discussion. A big emphasis on mindfulness and going toward that which you are rejecting—to note what you are avoiding. We spent about 10 minutes going over five questions from her end-of-year review. The questions we answered were:

~ Reader Feedback ~

One of the most exciting things about reading the tranquility du jour blog is seeing tiny wisps of "what if" become grand adventures. Kimberly never seems to forget her dreams . . . even as she balances businesses, charities, graduate school, and good and bad days. While she makes everyday grunt work a little brighter with fresh flowers, green tea, playtime with pets, and a good book, Kimberly waits patiently to pounce on long-hoped-for opportunities when they finally appear . . . the chance to open her own yoga studio{s}, to rescue animals in need, to travel to mythical places {while wearing clothes she designed herself!} and to teach others to look inside themselves and to become the architects of their own lives.

The blog made me start to wonder . . . what if I gave myself permission to fulfill some of my own lifelong dreams? For years I pictured going to law school on the West Coast—and this year I finally did! I followed Kimberly's example and tried pouring my personality into my reinvented life. This new project aligns my love of big, boring books, solving mysteries, and social justice for animals. As I head to school each morning with a thermos full of chai and reading glasses bought in Paris, my brain might complain, "this is really hard work!" and my heart replies, "but it's awesome!"

Darca, Canada

How have I spent my time?

What are results of these actions?

What realizations have I had over the past 12 months?

What has inspired me?

What are the blessings, sorrows, and disappointments? How have they changed me?

She shared a lot of Rumi poetry and challenged us to change a behavior pattern for three months. In her book she gives the example of no longer drinking wine after work. We can identify with certain behaviors intensely and break their impact on our world as a whole. Still pondering which one{s} I will change.

Also pondering the notion of simple living {less stuff} and less online time.

Sunday was a wrap-up day and I began my journey home. Although the workshop wasn't fully what I'd expected {thought there would be more product via reflection and less process}, I enjoyed the experience. My takeaways were:

1. Read more Rumi/poetry.
2. Infuse mindfulness into every day.
3. Explore what I avoid.
4. I've spent my time doing. Want to spend more time being.
5. Animals, travel, art journaling, time with family and friends, flowers, yoga inspire me.
6. Slow down and savor experiences at hand.
7. Change a behavior pattern for three months.
8. Any time something comes out of your mouth about another person, it is a reflection of you. Be aware. {Uh oh!}

It was a treat to meet Sarah in person and to dive into a practical exploration of mindfulness mixed with psychology. Her book was transformative for me this year, and I look forward to applying more of the principles. May we all embrace mindfulness in all we do.

4. CHANGE HAPPENS
July 2012

It's been a big week. Between ended relationships to job changes to moves, it seems as if each day has brought a new life change to loved ones around me. Everywhere I turn I'm hearing news of large transitions. Apparently these things come in waves and we're currently experiencing a tsunami in my neck of the woods.

Considering our interconnectedness, it's hard not to feel the effects of big changes happening to those you love and to begin to feel a bit unstable yourself. Change is filled with trepidation and lots of vacillating between should I or shouldn't I?

My semi-sabbatical has allowed me space to ponder change and to observe shifts around me. From people to nature to my pets. For example, I've been keenly aware of the changes in my patio garden and how the trees are flourishing in the summer sun! You know, the little things that happen each day as we're living our oh-so-busy lives. Life is change.

Since downshifting a bit {my inbox is half its size these days}, I've learned a few lessons in change that I've shared below.

1. **Know that change is part of life's process**. We are constantly evolving, growing, pruning, shedding. It's a good thing, even though it can be painful.

2. **Give yourself space to turn within and see what is or isn't working**. A few hours, a few days, a few weeks. Whatever you can muster. Your soul requires it. Autopilot is sad and overrated.

3. **Sit with what comes up**. Listen to your gut. Write about your feelings. When you have the answer, take action. Don't rush the process. Bask in it.

> Everything changes. Nothing remains without change.
> —Buddha

4. **Serve up support**. Indulge in self-care and offer support to those around you. Nothing is permanent. The pain will lessen and the storm will pass. Ride these waves *sans* attachment.

5. **Be gentle**. Have patience with yourself and the process. Feel your feelings. Be open to the journey. Explore opportunities and give yourself wiggle room. You're human and doing the best you can.

Ah, the journey of life. As John Lennon said, "Life is what happens while you are busy making other plans." Avoid autopilot, embrace change, and repot yourself from time to time. Yep, just as we do our houseplants.

5. BLOOM INTO BEING
March 2013

Spring has sprung. I'm ready! *Et toi?* Blooming trees, peonies, open windows, yoga on the deck, colorful impatiens, and chirping birds. These are just a few of the many things *j'adore* about this time of the year.

When I contemplate how I want to *be* this spring {lord knows I already have my long to-do list}, I'm reminded of this great article by Alva Noe titled *Are You Overwhelmed? You Don't Have to Be*. I love this line, "The bottom line seems to be that we know too much, understand too little and we are way too scared of what we might be missing." Does this resonate?

This reminds me of another insightful article from *The New Tork Times*, *The Busy Trap*.

The author writes, "Busyness serves as a kind of existential reassurance, a hedge against emptiness; obviously your life cannot possibly be silly or trivial or meaningless if you are so busy, completely booked, in demand every hour of the day." Hmmmm.

As we move into this season focused on blooming, I encourage you to take time to reflect on *how* you want to bloom. For *moi*, I'm hoping for deeper listening, full-bodied experiences, and more being. And the great news is I feel it slowly happening deep inside. It's a good feeling.

Wishing you a beautiful day filled with dreams of blooming into being.

6. SILENT MEDITATION RETREAT
May 2013

After a weekend basking in mindfulness {versus donning a black robe to receive my diploma}, I'm filled with gratitude for the mindfulness immersion. A truly decadent adventure.

During our free time {when we weren't in sitting meditation, walking meditation, eating vegan/gluten-free, hiking, doing yoga, listening to dharma talks and sharing}, I was reading from Phillip Moffit's book, *Dancing with Life*, or Soren Gordhamer's book, *Wisdom 2.0*. Both are incredibly juicy and I find myself slowly savoring Moffit's {more heady} while devouring Gordhamer's {more accessible}.

There are a few gems that spoke to me over the weekend. I wanted to pass this along to you from *Wisdom 2.0*:

For those of us who seek to live consciously and with less stress, it helps to align the internal and external, to see if our external actions do justice to what internally matters to us . . . If asked, I would answer that my health, eating well, and spending time in nature mattered, but my actions said otherwise. If you watched my actions, these were not at all my priorities. By my actions, what most mattered to me was knowing if I had received any messages in the two minutes since I had last checked. That is how I spent much of my day. This disconnect, I realized, was adding difficulty to my life. I thus had to either change what mattered to me or change my actions. By feeling one thing internally while my actions expressed completely different priorities, my life was out of alignment. In this situation, the very things that were truly important to me like my health and well-being, were not being addressed.

This reminded me of something Robin Fisher

Roffer shared in *Tranquility du Jour* podcast #244 about making changes when noticing her actions weren't aligning with her values. Her comment was a powerful reminder to regularly reflect and re-align. Over and over again.

As you review your to-do lists, appointments, relationships, and obligations, consider this post and the alignment of internal and external. I promise to continually do the same.

7. SMELL THE ROSES
June 2013

Bonjour from my window seat writing desk where light pink peonies from yesterday's farmers' market brighten my view. The day began with two big chilly rainstorms and now the temperature is expected to rise to 84. Gotta love Paris weather. Constant flux. Like life.

While smelling flowers along the *Promenade plantée* Saturday, my friend Denise captured me in my element. The rose was stunning. Layers of soft pink that looked like tissue paper. And they were everywhere. A true delight.

While stopping to smell the roses is, well, a tad *cliché*, there is an important lesson that lies within it. There is always something to complain about—weather, temperature, noise, hunger, thirst—or something else to rush off and handle. The repetitive notion of "if only things were X, then I would be happy." I hear this in my own head and out of the mouths of others often. It's this constant seeking of perfection.

If only it wasn't so hot, then this picnic would be perfect. If only my guests would mingle more, then the dinner party would be perfect.

If only I'd left the house 10 minutes earlier, then this traffic wouldn't be an issue. And on and on.

Why can't we simply savor the beauty in front of us versus wishing things were different? I ask myself this question often, too.

Today take a look around your home, office, or café {wherever you're reading this}, and find something to celebrate. Is it the tea you're sipping? The view you have? Your pretty nail color? The music you hear? Can you slow down what you're doing to embrace this very moment?

Moments are fleeting, leaving only sweet memories. Can you slow down to savor life and make time for what matters most? Only you have the power to make this happen. I'm rooting for you and trying to do the same. Let's stop and smell the roses.

8. PERFECTION
August 2013

While having lunch with friends recently, one noticed a ring on my finger that I wear from time to time. When she asked if it was new, I explained that I couldn't always wear it because sometimes it made my eczema flare up. "Ah," one exclaimed, "So you're not perfect!" Hmmm, that off-the-cuff comment has stayed with me for weeks. *Perfect? Oh Lordie, far from it. Let me count the ways.*

I often have a potty mouth. I've had a sugar addiction of sorts for years. I'm a mess in the kitchen. I've only read 50% of the books on my overflowing shelves. I need to sleep more than the average person. I'm an absolute wallflower in situations where I don't know anyone. Perfection? Ha!

I could go on, but I think you get the point. We aren't perfect beings and our messiness makes us a bit more, well, interesting. At least I like to think so.

What is perfection today? Maybe the woman who juggles family, carpools, career, organic eating, relationships, social obligations, and philanthropy—all while staying trim, in love, and gleefully happy.

Who knows? Honestly, perfection is probably

incredibly personal and where many struggles start, such as eating disorders. We see another's life and think how perfect it must be.

One thing I've learned over the years is not to compare my insides to anyone else's outsides. Ponder this one for awhile. It's a juicy statement.

Today observe your relationship with perfectionism. And know you are perfectly imperfect. Promise.

9. DIGITAL DAY OFF
December 2013

When I woke up yesterday in the woods of West Virginia, I knew I needed to treat it differently. Rather than reaching for my iPhone to "make sure everything is ok," I resisted and declared it a digital day off. After scanning my Sunday to-dos in my *Daybook*, I realized a few items needed online connection. And they could wait.

What else to do? Well, reading required my iPad, and I would be oh-so-tempted to peek at email. So I secured my eye pillow and curled up in the fetal position. I promptly went back to sleep savoring the sound of rain.

When I woke up later, I considered and pondered where to begin and considered my self-imposed limitations. I confessed to Le Beau that I felt my superpower had been removed. Then I wandered a bit, made a cuppa tea, once again reviewed my to-dos to see what didn't require getting online, and settled in to pen 2013 review/2014 dreams.

The results were joyful. Other than snapping three pictures through Instagram {that posted to Twitter} and looking at two texts that came in, I was blissfully in the moment. I practiced yoga, sat in meditation for 15 minutes, sipped my first organic hot cocoa with homemade marshmallows of the season, watched a delightful film {*Frances Ha*}, and played for hours in my art journal and *Daybook*.

However, it wasn't all sunshine and bunnies. I was detoxing. A few times each hour I would notice that twinge. The longing to see what was happening on Facebook, Instagram, or in my inbox. It's a powerful twinge! And as with many longings {hello pumpkin pie}, if you ignore it, it will subside. I know that sounds so basic, but it's true.

When on the train this morning heading back to D.C., I checked email and was relieved to see there were no emergencies yesterday. The world kept turning and life was well-lived.

Mindfulness is about observation, not judgment. The next time you feel that twinge, notice if you can resist {especially if enjoying the company of another}. Set designated times to check technology. Take time away from the screen. It will do you {and those around you} good.

10. PAUSE
February 2014

On the second leg of my flight from Oklahoma back to D.C., I returned to a book I've been savoring like a fine wine, *Manage Your Day-to-Day: Build Routine, Find Your Focus, and Sharpen Your Creative Mind*. I know, not your average "Oh, I can't wait to read what comes next" text, but it has been for me. Never said I was normal.

Within the book is a powerful essay called *Reclaiming Our Self-Respect* by James Victore stuck with me. He writes, "Busywork pulls our attention from the meaningful work—taking time to think, reflect, and imagine. Yet it's these pauses that make our lives better and lay the groundwork for our greatest accomplishments."

He went on to write, "Just as we watch our intake of caffeine or candy or alcohol lest we become addicted, we need to consciously develop a healthy relationship with our tools—or we lose perspective and become slaves to them." This is all in relation to what he describes as "our convenient connections," such as smartphones and social media which prevent us from being fully present.

While in Oklahoma I found myself posting heaps of pics on Instagram and checking my phone more often than I'd like. It's a fine balance between capturing the moment to share and being fully in the moment with the people around you. And it's a balance I continue to struggle with mastering.

Thus, my last day was declared a digital day off until I got to the airport at 5:00 p.m. and sent text messages that I was boarding. Then into the inbox I peeked. Delighted to see not a thing needing urgent attention—and to have broken the cycle of checking in when there is a lull or transition. Why not simply savor said lull or transition?

As you start this final week in February, consider your relationship to your tools {social media, smartphones, food, exercise, libations, TV}. Do you have perspective? Can you be alone with your thoughts? Are you mindfully or mindlessly consuming? Can you stand in line or wait for a bus without pulling out your smartphone for entertainment?

Remember, it's in those pauses that the magic happens. Let's pause today, tomorrow, and the next day, too. And to make this easier, the sun is beginning to shine longer, brighter, and with more warmth. I like to believe we're gearing up for spring blooming. Get outside and savor a sacred moment *sans* smartphone. Preferably with a four-legged friend in tow.

MINDFULNESS NUGGETS

1. Mindfulness is moment-to-moment nonjudgmental awareness.

2. Practice being imperfectly perfect.

3. Try a regular digital detox.

~ MINDFULNESS TAKEAWAYS ~

CHAPTER 9: Travel

We travel, some of us forever, to seek other states, other lives, other souls.
— Anaïs Nin

As I boarded the train at *Gard du Nord* en route to the country for a birthday celebration with friends, a smile washed over my face. There was a meowing cat, a few barking dogs, and hoards of people settling into their seats. As usual, I chose a window seat and dropped in for two hours of window gazing. With only a bottle of Veuve Cliquot, basic toiletries, and a change of clothes in a straw bag, I was off on an adventure.

Next I inserted ear buds and hit play as hip-hop artists serenaded at an obscene volume. My monkey mind began to quiet. Those two hours daydreaming to Eminem and Kanye proved to be an effective processing practice and put my 41st birthday in perspective. And the passing French landscape didn't hurt.

Escaping to another place offers a chance to reframe, regroup, and take it all in on a different frequency.

Over the past decade I've sought many travels to teach, learn, and explore. According to Pico Iyer, "We travel, initially, to lose ourselves, and we travel next, to find ourselves. We travel to open our hearts and eyes. And we travel, in essence, to become young fools again—to slow time down and get taken in, and fall in love once more."

Inside this chapter you'll find a piece on a retreat in Mallorca, Spain, observations in Paris, my Paris packing list, Tranquility Tour memories, the importance of culling experiences along the way, and more.

Tune into Tranquility du Jour podcasts #28, #204, #276 for more insights on travel.

> **~ READER FEEDBACK ~**
>
> Finding this blog was really the start of a reinventing of my life and my priorities. After enduring an abusive childhood {from which I was diagnosed with PTSD} and entering and ending a relationship with a man just like my stepfather, I knew I needed to change my mindset and my life.
>
> I had always believed that I was not creative or interesting and that I would only ever be good at school. But that didn't stop me from wanting creativity, confidence, and a chance to take charge of my life. *Tranquility du Jour* has given me the guidance and the tools to do just that.
>
> You can't underestimate the power of creating a life that is uniquely yours and full of the activities you love doing. And to express myself through being genuine and honest has always been my goal. *Tranquility du Jour* is that one blog for me that changed my life. It came into my life when I desperately needed it and showed me that it is okay to be me.
>
> *Tranquility du Jour* launched my self-exploration. I've learned so much about myself and what I love from Kimberly's experiences and wisdom. She also connected me with other artists and influential people. This blog truly started everything for me and I will be forever grateful for finding it.
>
> Melissa Cornwell, Vermont
> theinformationdojo.com

1. MUSINGS ON MALLORCA
November 2006

Returning to the magical island of Mallorca renewed my sense of self, purpose, and plans. I first explored Mallorca during a two-week solo vacation to celebrate my 30th birthday. This time I returned to honor the fruition of my book and a long-term dream. My time in Deia, a place made famous by novelist Robert Graves and the numerous artists and writers who followed, was picture perfect.

I arrived Wednesday night after 24 hours of traveling to a dark, but tranquil villa. The majority of the group had arrived and were chatting around a table in the outside garden. Despite being the only American, I immediately felt at home.

The first day we explored our various roles, values, and the masks that we wear. I spent the afternoon down time exploring a nearby town with my newfound Finnish friend.

The second day began with a two-hour Kundalini yoga session and a lecture on the six-fold path of well-being. Namely, mind, food, exercise, Vitamin O {oxygen}, relaxation, and meditation. I spent the afternoon napping. Our evening session included a lecture on herbs from a local expert and the sharing of a poem we were to have written during down time. I'll spare you my lack of poetic prose. I read it to Le Beau, and he said it sounded like an '80s hair band ballad.

The third day focused on emotional intelligence and how our emotions create our thoughts. This day got quite intense and the facilitator took us deeper. For example, we explored the concept of the shadow self and how we project our shadow onto others. She encouraged us to ask ourselves "What is it about them that I've got to learn?" The statement that 85% of leadership success is based on our EQ—how we manage emotions of self and others—really struck a chord. She also emphasized self-control by choosing the appropriate response to emotions and creating space before responding.

The fourth day we focused on fun creative play, beginning with sketching ourselves in 7-year increments. My only change was hair color from 7 to 14 to 21 to 28 to now. Then we practiced blind drawing and continual drawing techniques. The afternoon was spent in silence working on our visionary collage. In the evening we had a bonfire where we were to throw into the fire what we were giving up or shedding. I tend to be very practical in these exercises, as I know that it isn't as simple as throwing a piece of paper into the fire and POOF, certain things are gone. So I simply noted some simple changes I'd love to make —weekly solitude time, go to bed earlier and to rise, carve out grocery shopping time, set a nice table, have meal times with Le Beau, and incorporate more creative play.

The final day was a focus on action steps. I'm the queen of action steps so this was a fun day after loads of inner work and play. We shared our visionary collage with our assigned buddies and they were to present our vision to the group. I was blessed with the perfect fit buddy from the beginning and we resonated on many levels. My collage was filled with images of things I love—French pedicures, hot cocoa with whipped cream, stargazer lilies, waterfalls, yoga, meditation, bathtub soaking, beaches, couple time, fresh fruit and veggies. The focus was clear, more being time. Although my goal for the retreat had been to get clarity on business development, what emerged was a need to focus more on being rather than doing. I spent the afternoon gallivanting in nearby Soller and visiting a huge church, which brought about an immediate sense of peace. The evening culminated in sharing our action steps, and then dancing for three hours. We got all gussied up. Some of us donned wigs {mine was a long blue bob}, and had a wonderful evening of celebration.

The following day was bittersweet as I was one of the last to leave and said goodbye to new friends throughout the day. I spent some time at the Robert Graves museum, interviewed Lynne Franks {*Tranquility du Jour* podcast #57}, sipped tea in the village while discussing visionary work with a fellow participant, and then hopped in a cab for the airport. The drive to the airport was sad. I knew the experience had come to an end and we were all heading back to our regular routines. All the women were such gems, powerful entrepreneurs, and incredibly loving beings. The sun was setting as we drove the 45 minutes to Palma, and I kept peering out of the window until I could no longer see the town. The island of Mallorca has offered me many lessons over the years.

2. SENSORY BLISS
June 2012

Bonjour from Castellane, France, outside the famous Gorges du Verdon {aka Grand Canyon of Europe}. Today I drove from Gordes {a hillside gem} to *L'Occitane* factory and museum {loved learning about their foundation}, through hairpin turns requiring "nerves of steel" {as described in our travel book} in Gorges du Verdon. Lordie, it was SO pretty, but with my sweaty palms and racing heart, I didn't dare snap pics. My loss, but I'm happy to share that we are all in one piece many hair-raising hours later. And, I did need two glasses of *rosé* to decompress. Honestly, I think I'm still decompressing and will sleep like a baby tonight.

We've been fairly wifi-free the past many days. Our data stick is out, and wifi access doesn't always work on my computer {where I prefer to blog} ,so we've been reliant on random cafés for access. Thus, I've been able to post occasional photos on Instagram and Facebook, but not truly sit down and pen thoughts.

This journey has been one of a lifetime for sure. Rather than relying on train schedules or hotels that may not allow Le Pug {boo, dogists}, we rented a camper to see Provence as it offered more freedom. We've enjoyed campgrounds in the mountains, on the beach, and in parking lots with luxuries of electricity, a stove {must-have for hot tea}, double bed, toilet and sinks.

Confession: for years I've longed to rent a camper and travel across the US, but each time we looked into it, between gas and the rental, it was well beyond our budget. Thus, when exploring how to bask in our two weeks off in Provence, this felt like a win-win {and a generous birthday gift from Le Beau = *merci*!}. Downside = the camper is HUGE, especially by my small pink bike standards, has no rear window and requires Le Beau to get out and direct when we need to reverse. It's challenging to maneuver in small French towns, although we've only gotten stuck once so far.

Over the past week and a half I've done heaps of reading, a bit of writing and napping, lots of experiencing, and sprinkles of big picture thinking. No big epiphanies, but I know seeds have been planted from various readings and experiences. It's been a joy to let go, to have limited access to the online world, and be immersed in this part of the world filled with a plethora of sensory bliss.

The French relish downtime and nurturing the senses. Most of the country is closed on Sunday. While in Salon de Provence, I opened my laptop at a café to write while Le Beau ran an errand. For nearly 30 minutes I didn't get served. When I requested a menu, the waiter said he didn't want to distract my work and to put my computer away to enjoy the day. Wow, well okay! I wasn't "working" per se, but enjoying the flow of my thoughts. However, it's not the norm in France to see people with a laptop at a café. When in Rome . . . .

I'm grateful to have this opportunity to bask in Provence. This region is known for its lavender, good food, and sunshine. It's given us that and much, much more. Le Pug has loved the adventure, and has been quite the trooper, Le Beau has been a loving travel companion and navigator, and this region has offered me the opportunity to regroup after hosting two ten-day retreats.

It's hard not to feel tranquil when you fall asleep to sounds of crickets under starry nights with gentle breezes . . . When fed the most succulent fruits and vegetables . . . When gazing out over lush vistas seen previously on postcards . . . When inhaling the scent of lavender . . . When hanging freshly laundered clothes to dry . . . When savoring quiet moments in "legs up the camper" and in old churches.

We have a few days left in the camper, and the plan is to hit Grasse for perfumerie bliss before heading back to Paris via train for *mon anniversaire,* and then home late Sunday. I'll continue to process this experience, bask in it the few days we have left, and promise to bring you along for the ride. My plan is to incorporate this sensory bliss at home—more produce shopping at local markets, hanging clothes outside to dry, and more tea sipping *sans* technology.

3. INDIA HIGHLIGHTS
November 2012

A potpourri of experiences from my second jaunt to yoga's motherland:

- Giving tea biscuits to shunned street dogs and hungry sacred cows.
- Having ample time to write, edit, and rest. To bed by 6 p.m. some nights.
- Picking up heaps of holiday treats from local artisans and small business owners.
- Meeting my new 8-year-old beau Arjun, along with his parents and sweet sisters.
- Indulging in yummy organic food and good work at Ramana's Garden.
- Taking and teaching yoga with new friends.
- Donning my hot pink sari and having it re-wrapped by many Indian women along the way to aarti {apparently I need lessons}.
- Seeing monkeys. I still squeal like a little girl every time. Love, love, love them!
- Singing kirtan and feeling the vibrations of the chants throughout my being.
- Taking a boat ride across the Ganges.
- Hiking to a beautiful waterfall with a friend from San Diego. We met in Costa Rica last year and reunited during Rishikesh travels at aarti. Small world.
- Being dropped off and picked up by Le Beau and Le Pug.
- Sipping heaps of lemon ginger honey and Masala tea. Yum!
- Oh, and did I mention feeding the dogs and cows? I know, I know, but such joy they bring *moi*!

4. GLAMPING
May 2013

Bonjour from Starbucks in Dupont Circle, where I'm stationed for a dose of green tea and splash of wifi. This week has been one of excitement, new experiences, and an ongoing return to the present moment. Inhale, exhale.

I'm over the moon that we've found the perfect tiny {20-foot} home for our upcoming Tranquility Tour. The camper was on Craigslist.com and we purchased it from a sweet 75-year-old, Meryl, who wore boots and a combed-over head of colored dark brown hair.

Since procuring the camper, there have been many experiences . . . From sitting at the West Virginia DMV for two hours {and debating much-too-heavily between the wildlife or breast cancer awareness plate}; to camping and trying to contain three pets who want to run into the woods when the camper door opens; to outfitting our new vintage camper with "essentials" such as soft linens, peppermint candles, LED lighting, handmade bunting, and a tea kettle; to walking to the Metro from the campground through the woods today.

Oh, and let us not forget the constant demands for food {just today claustrophobic Le Beau was pinned in at 5 a.m. by hungry kitties}. The cherry on top, the kitties have to be watched when consuming food lest a "starving" pug swoop in and consume it all with one gulp.

We will be doing some updates to the 1988 interior, which has more of a '70s vibe. To start, we plan to paint the wood-paneled interior white to brighten it up. I'll get Mama Wilson going on toile, damask, or chevron curtains and coordinating slipcovers for the cushions. Sadly, not sure that a chandelier is going to be possible, but I'll keep pushing. These simple

edits will brighten it up and add a dollop of charm. The outside needs a splash of pink, and we're still mulling over the exterior transformation.

I've been on a camper kick for years. Both sets of grandparents had Airstream trailers, and I loved playing clubhouse in them. In 2011 I began looking for my own Airstream clubhouse online and have dabbled with the idea heavily over the past two years. Why? I needed a girly place to play and create at Le Beau's masculine cabin in the woods. When we came up with the Tranquility Tour concept, we knew it was time to get serious about finding the perfect fit. Although my initial dream was for a trailer, we would have had to purchase two new-to-us used vehicles versus one. Thus, the stand-alone camper decision. Oh, and it will serve as the perfect fashion truck for TranquiliT, too.

There are many darling books about glamour camping {coined glamping} and living a nomadic lifestyle. As I walked off the deck this morning carrying my suitcase to the camper in clogs, I embraced a not-so-glamorous moment slumped over on the ground. I'm sure there will be *many* more.

This vintage camper has been a longtime dream. It's a delight to have it come true within our tiny budget. By pinpointing dreams, creating a budget, searching and waiting for the perfect fit, plus having a plan, dreams come to life in due time.

What dreams do you have lying within? Well, it's a new month and time to pen May dreams. Why not plant a bold seed into your *Tranquility du Jour Daybook*? Begin watering it with attention and intention this month—and beyond. You may surprise yourself.

~ LET'S RETREAT ~

I love silence. I love time alone. I love contemplation. A retreat is like a weeklong slumber party for the soul.

How to retreat:

1. **Find the perfect setting**: Picnic at a park, week on the West Coast, day at the beach, month abroad.

2. **Secure travel arrangements**: Car rental, cab pick up, hotel or apartment, flight.

3. **Set expectations**: Let loved ones know you're away and work colleagues know your availability.

4. **Pack lightly**: Lots of layers, camera, journal, pens, leave ample room for returning with goodies for family and friends.

5. **Craft an intention**: What are you seeking through this journey?

6. **Leave footprints + love**: Connect with all beings you meet along the path with respect and admiration.

7. **Return with treats**: A poem you penned, coffee from a plantation visit, locally made taffy.

5. PARIS PACKING LIST
May 2013

As I prepare to leave the country tonight for France, I'm pulling together my favorite pieces to mix and match. **Below is my packing list for six weeks away:**

Seven bottoms
Five tops
Four dresses {three can also be worn as tunics over pants}
A few accessories
Lingerie
Socks
Art supplies
Books
iPad + MacBook Air
Chargers
Daybook
Three pairs of shoes
Toiletries
Earplugs + eye mask
Vitamins
Reusable bags
Printouts of tickets
Sunnies
Eyeglasses
Universal adapter
Reusable tea thermos + water bottle
Tights
= *voilà*, almost ready to go!

Bottoms:
Palazzo pants*
Striped skirt dress*
Dark denim jeans
Parisian pants*
Shiny leggings
Parisian skirt*
Lounge short*

Tops:
Vintage denim jacket
Long sleeve wrap tunic*
2in1 chemise*
Cardigan
2in1 fitted top*

Dresses:
Long slip dress
3/4 sleeve wrap dress*
2in1 slip dress*
Vintage slip

Accessories:
Three scarves
Two reusable bags for jaunts to farmers' markets
Long faux pearls
Vintage sparkly earrings

Miscellaneous:
Woven tote
Black clogs
Silver ballet flats
Pink Converse sneakers
Vintage suitcase filled with art supplies
Leopard-print yoga mat
Leopard-print umbrella

Au revoir. I'll be back in touch once I'm in my beloved City of Light.

* from TranquiliT.com

Anthology Extras: Lessons à la New York City
August 2011

Since our arrival Friday afternoon, we've been in sprint mode to see and do everything possible. It's the New York City way. Yoga, vegan lunches, vintage shopping, Betsey Johnson fragrance launch, flea markets, bookstores, and meet-ups. This city is an absolute joy in so many ways. I've snapped heaps of photos that serve as design, window display, and style inspiration. Thank gawd for the iPhone.

Le Beau and I dropped Le Pug at a dog spa today for a little doggie indulgence and have been working at Starbucks ever since. It's been good to get a little grounded and reconnected after days of running all over the city. As we prepare to dash out for a meeting, I wanted to share tips from my past few days:

1. **Wear comfy shoes.** I've walked miles here so far!
2. **Stay hydrated.** Always tote your water bottle or yummy libation.
3. **Smile at strangers.**
4. **Hit flea markets** on the last day for better bargains.
5. **Always don your game face.** You never know whom you'll run into.
6. **Craft a casual meet-up.** Met such such beautiful souls at our *Tranquility du Jour* blog meet-up Monday night.
7. **Take time to retreat from over-stimulation.** My chest begins to feel crushed among the chaos {like simply walking down the sidewalk}. A little yoga and retreating does the soul good.
8. **Don layers** to combat the overly airconditioned locales and adjust for rain and sunshine.
9. **Carry a camera at all times.** There is inspiration everywhere.
10. **Carry your journal and/or ideas book** to meetings to capture inspiration and ideas.

6. EXPERIENCES
May 2013

Bonjour from Paris. Retreat number one begins this afternoon with an "Impressionists of Paris" boat cruise on the Seine, departing from the Eiffel Tower. *Ooh la la.* I'm over the moon about this brand-new offering and can't wait to bask in the many sensory experiences Paris will offer our yoga, art + shopping retreaters {and *moi*}.

While waiting to board the flight Monday night, a fellow retreater asked if there was anything I wanted to purchase in Paris. I responded that I wasn't seeking a thing. She proclaimed, "Oh, you're focusing on experiences." Indeed I am, but I hadn't put two and two together before she stated such.

Experiences, aren't they what life is all about? And Parisians tend to do this very well. I hope to take a page from their book. I couldn't wait for the farmers' market at the end of the block to open today so I could pick up fresh *fleurs* {hello lilacs and peonies} and fresh produce for an afternoon salad.

While I sit here writing, I'm filled with gratitude for this experience. The opportunity to work and write in Paris. The chance to fill my body with fresh food. The ability to hit pause and practice savoring. Interestingly, I just downloaded the book *Savor: Mindful Eating, Mindful Life*. As I approached the farmers' market today, I felt like a kid at Christmas. While washing the fresh lettuce, same feeling. While placing the flowers into vases, ditto.

Life is about creating experiences, not accumulating things. We know this, but do we practice this? Over the next few days I'll be art journaling and sharing my goals for this Paris jaunt. My plan is to have a large focus on experiences. And it began yesterday as I sipped my first pot of tea at a sidewalk café in the rain. Make today an experience.

Anthology Extras: Soul Longing
September 2013

Our big Tranquility Tour announcement in April was followed by heaps of planning, coordination, and dreaming. It's hard to believe the final days until takeoff are upon us. Yep, after our kickoff on Tuesday night, we'll head out to West Virginia, pack up our vintage camper, Miss Lillie, and head to New York. There we'll camp, savor the Wisdom 2.0 conference on mindfulness in business, and launch our first Tranquility Pop-Ups in Philly and Brooklyn.

Since my kitty Bonnard's passing in July, we've decided to leave our second senior rescue kitty, Matisse, at home where he'll be happier. Unlike Bonnard who loved the open road, Matisse has never been much of a traveler. Instead of three pets, we'll simply have Le Pug gracing us with his presence. Funny how things can change so quickly, and I'm trying my best to learn to go with the ever-changing flow.

In 1997, I took three months to travel from D.C. to Alaska and down the West Coast in an SUV. Camping, sleeping in the car, and savoring an occasional soak in a hotel tub. For the past 15 years, I've been committed to long-term projects such as creating and growing Tranquil Space plus completing grad school programs and various trainings. All the while, my wanderlust has been tucked in my back pocket awaiting attention.

I would often tell Le Beau that my birthday wish would be to travel cross-country in a camper for two weeks. Funny how I couldn't see past a two-week adventure. Gas and rental costs were always prohibitive so this dream, too, remained tucked away.

After spending two weeks in a camper exploring Provence last year, I realized that away time didn't have to be in two-week spurts and that my wanderlust wishes were still strong despite being ignored for so long. *Be responsible. Focus on growing and improving. What will happen if you're away for so long?* These are just some of the voices in my head ensuring that I didn't escape beyond two weeks. It's the American way, after all.

The funny thing is that I now see how quickly the two months will pass. Our 11,000-mile schedule is quite tight considering our extensive route. However, I'm hopeful there will be many more adventures to come in sweet Lillie. And hopefully many more adventures in general. I don't want my legacy to be "she worked hard and did the conventional thing."

~ READER FEEDBACK ~

Reading your blog and myriad messages made me feel lighter, fresh, and comforted. It/you made me smile and take a break, and sometimes tear up. Often you held up a mirror and I saw myself in you or the self I had wanted to be; both reminders of my past and better, future possibilities. In sharing your personal and business experiences, you expanded my mind. It/you opened an inner door and welcomed me inside to cultivate the beauty that is found everywhere. Together through cyberspace, you spawned thoughts that brought me back from disregard or non-awareness to being present and receptive. *Et il est la!*

Kimberly Wulfert, PhD, California
KimberlyWulfert.com

Day in. Day out. I want it to be something larger—involving innovation, charting a new course, and making some sort of meaningful difference.

Thus, as you can see, this tour means so much more to me than simply getting out of town for two months. It's a message. A message to my soul that it hasn't been forgotten. A message to blog readers and podcast listeners that I can't wait to meet you. A message to everyone that the world keeps turning even if you step off the hamster wheel. A message to you that it's good to shake things up from time to time and do something different, unexpected, or "irresponsible." A message of spreading the work of Farm Sanctuary and Tranquil Space Foundation—the tour's two beneficiaries.

Can't wait to connect on this adventure that means so much to my soul. See you in person, in spirit, or online as we share the journey far and wide. What sort of conventions do you hold while your soul longs for something else? Oh, to ponder! It's worth listening.

7. TRANQUILITY TOUR MONTH ONE
October 2013

As we handle laundry at our campground on a sexy Saturday night, I'm in awe that we've been on the road one month already. Being *sans* wifi during our time in Canada, it's a treat to be reconnected with a semblance of wifi at this Idaho campground. Semblance meaning a bit slower than dial-up. This month has been a complete joy with the overarching goal to be in the moment and capture a few via photos along the way. Here are some of our highlights to date.

Tranquility Tour Memories

Seeing lights from Ground Zero on 9/11 anniversary

Wisdom 2.0 conference

Sipping green juice with pal Baby B in NYC

Connecting with delightful podcast listeners + blog readers

Meeting Aussies in Brooklyn

8 delightful Tranquility Pop-Ups + 1 Meetup at Farm Sanctuary

Spending time with the animals at Farm Sanctuary

Lunch in Watkins Glen, NY, with Carol

Lillie's breakdown + repair

Poutine and playtime in Montreal with Jenn + Jason

Family time in New York

Soaking in a tub in Pittsburgh {*merci* Lexi}

Shipping books from the road

Pigs, glitter pumpkins + pink glory in Peoria, IL

Receiving the sweetest personalized gift bag for Le Pug from our friends at Zen Zone

Sleeping in style at rest stops

The smell of campfires

Donning only a few outfits {clothing in 12"x12" drawer}

Waving at closed national parks courtesy of the government shutdown

Crazy winds in Wyoming

Cheap hotel night in Calgary for a dose of wifi

Napping while Le Beau drives

Hurricane winds in Waterton National Park

Penning morning pages in my journal

Taping up sweet Lillie with damask duct tape

Devouring a box of Timbits

Savoring Kettle Korn popcorn by the campfire

Insane {Le Beau calls it irrational} fear of bears = toting bear spray everywhere

Sending love notes + packages from the road

Indulging at a tiny cowboy café in Idaho

Seeing first drops of snow in Jackson, Wyoming

Catching up on months of email fireside at a saloon

Reviewing your feedback from 2012 summer survey to help steer projects

Creating a glamping {glamour camping} haven within Miss Lillie

Editing of *Tranquility du Jour Daybook* for Monday's pre-sale

Doing laundry on a Saturday night at an RV "resort"

Finding old-timey ghost story podcasts

Listening to audio books

Warming by campfire

Reading by twinkle lights

Parking our bodies at Starbucks + McDonald's to support our wifi needs

Daydreaming out the window for hours

Savoring a grape slush from Sonic drive-in

Excited to see what this next month holds, and can't wait to meet more of you along the adventure. Thank you for being a part of this journey.

8. TWO MONTHS ON THE ROAD
November 2013

Friday night we'll park Miss Lillie at Le Beau's West Virginia cabin and return to D.C. Saturday, marking the end of our two-month Tranquility Tour. What an adventure we've had and my heart is full. Very full.

As I sat down to pen highlights, I'm in a slight state of shock that we've traveled 11,000 miles, met so many amazing people, seen such gorgeous landscapes, and that it comes to an end after Friday's final Tranquility Pop-Up in Richmond, Virginia. A shocking return to reality.

We'll be stationary. Living in a home *sans* wheels. With a tub and fireplace. I'll return to teaching my Monday and Thursday yoga + meditation classes plus specialty workshops and charity classes at Tranquil Space. Le Beau will return to his role at Tranquil Space in person {he's been overseeing from the road}. And we'll return to making the Pink Palace our haven. Just in time for the hollydaze.

Mid-October I shared some highlights from our first month on the road and here are some from this past month:

Tranquility Pop-Ups and Meetups in: Seattle, Portland, San Francisco, Monterey, Santa Barbara, Los Angeles, Farm Sanctuary, San Diego, Phoenix, Amarillo, Oklahoma, Greensboro

Time with the Redwoods

Biking with Le Pug in a basket among the Redwoods

Petting pigs at Farm Sanctuary

The Walk for Farm Animals in Los Angeles

Reading *Still Writing, The New Good Life,* and *Ooh La La*

Hiking in Muir Woods

Gazing at stars

Tea time at Samovar Tea Lounge

Visiting the Henry Miller Memorial Library

Visiting the Johnny Cash Museum + singing along at a Nashville honky tonk

Dining at Google

Traveling along the Pacific Coast Highway

Savoring an insanely delicious cinnamon roll + black rose tea at a Big Sur café

Getting a few miles from the Mexican border in Arizona

Making 150 lavender cactus jelly gifts in Oklahoma

Biking along the Grand Canyon rim

Sending over 60 love notes via snail mail

Camping in Joshua Tree National Park

Campfires at Marina Dunes, Redwoods, and Joshua Tree

Sunny turned chilly and windy beach time in the Outer Banks

Sitting fireside at a historic inn in Taos, New Mexico

Family time in Seattle, Portland + Oklahoma

Watching movies with Mom, Pops, Le Pug + Le Beau

Soaking in the claw foot tub in Oklahoma

Adopting a mountain lion for Pops and Tranquil Space

Days of watching the world pass by from the passenger seat

Tasting Indian fry bread again

As I begin to tie a bow around this two-month journey, I will continue penning takeaways in my journal, and will share them shortly. I believe there will be lots to process and a need to acclimate to civilian life *sans* wheels and traveling many miles a day.

In true Kimberly style I've booked myself solid upon return. Saturday afternoon hair appointment to enhance my roots. Check. {Pops stood over me in Oklahoma and proclaimed, "My, you've got lots of gray." I know, Pops. That's why I'm "blonde."} Returning to my Sunday morning meditation practice with a visiting friend. Check. Kennedy Center sent me {and thousands of other ballet fans} a special rate for the final showing of *Sleeping Beauty* on Sunday afternoon. Check. A friend comes over for dinner and a conference call Sunday evening. Check.

Although I'm sad this adventure is coming to an end, it's been a true journey of a lifetime. I feel incredibly blessed to have had the opportunity to travel far and wide with my two favorite boys in tow. While I let the experience marinate and return to daily life in the Pink Palace, Tranquil Space, and beyond, I look forward to carrying this newfound appreciation for living with less. Much less. Like my 1ft x 1ft clothing drawer.

Stay tuned for what will unfold from the Tranquility Tour journey. We'll be hosting a small show-and-tell at Tranquil Space—complete with photos and stories. It's been a true honor to spread the word about Tranquil Space Foundation and Farm Sanctuary. To meet you. And to share tools for tranquility while living among nature in a tiny vintage camper. I foresee myself returning refreshed and ready. For what? To be determined. *Always* to be determined.

9. TRANQUILITY TOUR TRIVIA
November 2013

Miles traveled: 11,525

Tanks of gas: 55

Average cost of tank: $80

Bath tub soaks: 4

Events hosted: 22

People met on tour: 183

Camper breakdowns: 1

Tires replaced: 4 plus spare

Max nights in one spot: 3 {in New York, Portland, Oklahoma, Lake Louise}

Olive Gardens visited: 3

Candles burned: 5

Cows petted: 3

States touched by Miss Lillie: 27

Pigs petted: 5

Provinces crossed: 4

Days on the road: 67

Brownies consumed: heaps

Hotel rooms: 3

Miles biked with Le Pug in bike basket: 1

Inns visited: 1 {in Taos}

Favorite spot: Redwoods/Avenue of the Giants {her}, Grand Canyon bike path {him}

First snow: Jackson, Wyoming

Spontaneous stops turned spiritual: Henry Miller Library + Johnny Cash museum

Average miles traveled per day: 172

Clothing: fit in 1sq. foot drawer {her}, fit in 1sq. foot cabinet {him}

Donation to charities: $2,500

Farm sanctuaries visited: 2 {New York + California}

Average amount spent per day: $184 {gas, campground, food}

Boxes of Hot Tamales consumed: 10

10. TRANQUILITY TOUR TAKEAWAYS
December 2013

This is a post I've thought about for a month, so I've decided to quit processing and start penning.

While camping in the Outer Banks in early November, I penned a few takeaways from my collaboration with Le Beau in my journal. Since I've been home, I've pondered the takeaways. When asked, I simply shared that I'm *still* processing the experience.

Truth is there are so many takeaways, yet they are so simple that I've struggled to put them all into a few nuggets. Here's my attempt to tie a bow around our 22-event, two-month, 11,500-mile Tranquility Tour with my top 10 Tranquility Tour takeaways:

1. **Live with less**: Honestly, living with a one-square-foot drawer for my clothing was no problem. Nor is living in 100 square feet of space with Le Beau and Le Pug. Or having one tote for my toiletries. I've been on a mission to purge since our return and feel no desire to shop for anything other than essentials/consumables {and a few books, of course}.

2. **I heart the open road:** Looking out the window for hours became my full-time job. And I liked it. Daydreaming is a worthy profession.

3. **Determine your essentials**: Sure, Le Beau scoffed at me for packing five candles, two tiny succulents, and white twinkle lights, but they added a nice touch. Some delights are simply non-negotiable.

4. **Home is where you make it**: Driving Miss Lillie on highways and then parking her into a campsite at night felt perfect. Within minutes we had twinkle lights plugged in, candles burning, and the bed unrolled. Only missing pieces were a fireplace and bathtub.

5. **Be with nature**: My favorite experiences were not so much the cities {even though I love them}, but the smell, sounds, and beauty of the great outdoors. I'm a city girl who needs regular time in the woods.

6. **Be prepared**: Picking up bear spray made me feel much more empowered in the Canadian Rockies. So. Very. Scared. I've skimmed too many bear attack books. Toting rain boots, an umbrella, sunscreen, a space heater, a wine opener, and other helpful sundries ensured we were set for various conditions.

7. **Being connected feels good**: Although I never missed home, having the chance to be in touch via social media, email, text, and phone helped me feel less away. I loved meeting long-time podcast listeners and blog readers, reconnecting with former Tranquil Space yogis, and seeing family. Interconnection rocks.

8. **Guilt was removed**: I often feel guilty for working on a project for one business and not working on another business or not being at the studio. It's something I've suffered from for years. Being on tour while raising money for Tranquil Space Foundation and spreading the word about *Tranquilologie* —while donning TranquiliT—was one of my first guilt-free two months in nearly 15 years. I continued blogging, podcasting, and teaching yoga with my two companions. It was all-encompassing.

9. **It feels good to be home**: We've been back in D.C. almost four weeks now, and I'm loving the sight of many familiar faces. The warm welcome we received made us feel so special. And returning with the hollydaze on the horizon has made it even more delightful.

10. **Slow is good**: Although we were constantly on the move, it was slow compared to modern day cross-country travel via plane. Sitting around the campfire, watching the rolling hills shift from tiny to large as we approached, toodling down the Pacific Coast Highway, biking along Grand Canyon's rim, and peering out the window for hours is good for the soul.

My overarching takeaways are: I loved, loved, loved meeting many of you. I love Miss Lillie {our vintage camper}. I loved being with Le Beau and Le Pug constantly for 9.5 weeks. I loved having a vehicle where I could use the loo and take a nap while Le Beau was driving down the highway. And, I look forward to many more adventures like this.

TRAVEL NUGGETS

1. Relish downtime and nurture your senses.

2. Cultivate experiences and live with less.

3. Listen to your wanderlust wishes.

~ TRAVEL TAKEAWAYS ~

CHAPTER 10.
Epilogue

Life is a process of becoming, a combination of states we have to go through. Where people fail is that they wish to elect a state and remain in it. This is a kind of death. — Anaïs Nin

A Decade

Reviewing posts from the past ten years has been an insightful peek into the evolution of this blog, my writing, and, ultimately, myself. Culling through a decade of photos, texts, quotes, and tips has illuminated an evolutionary process online and offline.

For example, I've gotten more comfortable in my skin. I now know that I require hours of recovery after being "on" and am better able to attend to my introversion. I've savored highs such as petting sanctuary pigs and celebrating Tranquil Space's 15th year—complete with red carpet and a Step and Repeat. I've weathered lows such as losing loved ones and feeling a lack of enoughness. I've slowed down and begun to whittle things out of my life on many levels. My writing practice has deepened, my message continues to crystallize, and my ongoing quest for tranquility remains strong.

Basic choices made daily offer a chance to enlighten and transform. Curl up with a good book. Watch an educational documentary. Try writing in your journal for 30 minutes without stopping. Turn on Madonna and dance around your living room. Invite someone over for tea. Sit on a non-profit board. Start a specialty group and host the first gathering. Pull out paint, ephemera, and stamps for an hour of play in your art journal. Lather yourself in French soap. Nurture a pet, plant, or garden with love. Eat veggies. Let yourself become. And become. Again and again.

Dancer and choreographer Twyla Tharp says, "I read for growth, firmly believing that what you are today and what you will be in five years depends on two things: the people you meet and the books you read." Since 2004 I've read heaps of books {and stockpiled many more} and met many new people—mainly a

courtesy of the blog and podcast. Thus, I'm hopeful that there has been, and will continue to be, obvious growth. Stay tuned.

Savvy Sources

As an avid reader—okay, bibliophile—I have go-tos that have served me well. No creation of mine is complete without a smattering of Savvy Sources.

For creativity, look no further than Julia Cameron's *The Artist's Way*. Wanting a crash course in business? Michael Gerber's *The E-Myth* is your book. Ready to go deep? Pick up Sarah Susanka's *The Not So Big Life*. Starting or growing a yoga practice? Try *Jivamukti Yoga* by Sharon Gannon and David Life. Grieving? *Grieving Mindfully* by Sameet Kumar helped me through a tough time. Craving more mindfulness? Jon Kabat-Zinn's *Wherever You Go, There You Are* is a must-have. Want to tame your time? *168 Hours* by Laura Vanderkam will help. Is writing a practice or a dream? Add Anne Lamott's *Bird by Bird*, Dani Shapiro's *Still Writing*, and William Zinsser's *On Writing Well* to your library. Curious about animals and food? Grab Gene Baur's *Farm Sanctuary*. Raring to increase your activism? Zoe Weil's *Most Good, Least Harm* will not disappoint. Wanting to feel French? Try Jennifer Scott's *Lessons from Madame Chic*.

And the cherry on top? Five of these authors have been interviewed on the *Tranquility du Jour* podcast, so you can get to know their work even better.

Big Pink Organza Bow

As we tie a pretty bow around the past ten years of *Tranquility du Jour*, I want to express extreme gratitude for reading along. Your comments, emails, and support has offered a sense of belonging to something that expands well beyond Washington, D.C. You've given me the space to grieve, celebrate, and muse publicly. For that, I'm eternally grateful.

As I fantasize about the next decade, I see a continual shift toward simplification with a sprinkle of adventure. There will be a memoir, a 50th birthday, a therapy license for private practice, and many, many returns to Paris. Beyond that, I'm open to what unfolds and striving to focus on the moment in front of me. It, and it only, deserves my utmost attention one breath at a time.

May we have another decade of becoming together—complete with piles of books, deep connections, and warm cups of rose tea. I bow to you, dear online community, for helping me feel whole, loved, and understood. You are beautiful and I am blessed.

Bisous, Kimberly

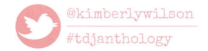

Anthology Extras: Awakening
August 2014

Ever since the Jewel song with lyrics, "You can be Henry Miller and I'll be Anaïs Nin, except this time it'll be even better, we'll stay together in the end," I've been slightly obsessed with their relationship. Actually, this song was my first introduction to them. Curious? There's a movie *Henry & June* that may shed light.

During my daily metro commute from Virginia into a D.C. law firm nearly 20 years ago, you'd find me curled up on the orange vinyl seats with a copy of Anaïs Nin diaries. Devouring them like a fine wine and dreaming of Paris in the '20s and '30s.

While in NYC for the Writer's Digest Conference last weekend, I came across this quote by Anaïs Nin and paused: "You live like this, sheltered, in a delicate world, and you believe you are living. Then you read a book . . . or you take a trip . . . and you discover that you are not living, that you are hibernating. The symptoms of hibernating are easily detectable: first, restlessness. The second symptom {when hibernating becomes dangerous and might degenerate into death}: absence of pleasure. That is all. It appears like an innocuous illness. Monotony, boredom, death. Millions live like this {or die like this} without knowing it. They work in offices. They drive a car. They picnic with their families. They raise children. And then some shock treatment takes place, a person, a book, a song, and it awakens them and saves them from death. Some never awaken." I even texted it to a few friends with a "whoa!" attached.

Ever sense you, too, may be hibernating? Sometimes I refer to this stage as germinating. You know, that feeling of something brewing underneath, but not quite ready to come to fruition? "Restlessness" and "absence of pleasure." What might awaken you?

In the hotel bar post-conference, I relished a birthday gift, *Labyrinth of Desire* by Rosemary Sullivan, while sipping my favorite wine, Chateau Ste. Michelle Riesling. This also brought about a pause. Juicy and well worth the read. She writes, "Love is a necessary obsession. But is it another we are searching for, or the missing half of ourselves?"

Sharing the Anaïs Nin quote and *Labyrinth of Desire* within Mindful Monday feels *apropos*. Why? Questioning whether things feel stuck or safe is necessary. It's more risky than the status quo. Is there a place, a person, a book, or a song that beckons you to awaken?

Only you know the answer.

Anthology Extras: Not Knowing
August 2014

While teaching recently, I came across beloved Pema Chödrön's recent book *Living Beautifully with Uncertainty and Change*. As I opened the text, I saw this quote by Agnes de Mille, "Living is a form of not being sure, not knowing what next or how. The moment you know how, you begin to die a little. The artist never entirely knows. We guess. We may be wrong, but we take leap after leap in the dark." Upon reading it, I exhaled. It was just what I needed to hear.

Despite the deep desire to plan and know my next move, life has a way of offering gentle, well, alternatives. Sometimes in the form of unplanned transitions, shifts, or options.

I find myself longing for obvious clarity on a regular basis. Almost as if there should be a message in the clouds crystallizing the next move.

It's a constant dance between planning and spontaneity. Being prepared and being surprised. Staying open and staying stuck.

My discomfort with not knowing has been a lifelong journey. I enjoy plans and knowing next steps in a calculated manner.

Over the years I've shared this angst here, and the "on my mind" post from July 2012 {on p. 114} is a perfect example. Freshly on my semi-sabbatical, feeling discombobulated after 13 years of pouring my soul into Tranquil Space, dealing with deep grief over the passing of my Gramma, and wondering what was next.

This wonder continues despite having a trajectory. Basking in not being sure, although uncomfortable, can be a delightfully fluid space.

There will be illness, loss, drought, hellos, and goodbyes along the way. Staying open to life's surprises encourages a softening of rigidity and an awakening to leaping in the dark.

~ TAKEAWAYS ~

Appendix

~ MONTHLY, WEEKLY + DAILY TRANQUILITY TOOLS ~

24 Tranquility Tools to enhance your
days, weeks, and months with meaningful tranquility.

8 Monthly Tools

1. craft month's dreams
At the start of each month, pull out your journal and pen your big dreams for the month. At the end of the month, review your list to give yourself a pat on the back for the items you were able to complete, and carry over the ones that remain and still feel close to your heart.

2. mani/pedi
Nurture your nails by adding a splash of color to match the season, trimming your cuticles, and savoring a bubbly foot bath. Or, indulge in another form of well-deserved self-care.

3. volunteer
Give a sampling of your resources—time, money, or energy—to a favorite cause and watch how you can have a powerful effect on others and your own well-being.

4. entertain
Invite a friend over for tea or host an intimate dinner fête for a few of your closest girlfriends. Don an apron, set the table, light candles, and channel your inner Martha Stewart.

5. review budget
Make sure that you aren't spending more than you are bringing in and set up a system for regular

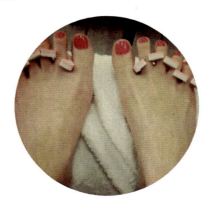

review. This doesn't have to be anything fancy—pencil and paper with a pile of receipts will do the trick! Or, go high tech with mint.com.

6. read two books
To ensure you are continually learning, growing, and expanding your horizons, read and finish two books monthly, and watch your consciousness grow. Read along with our online book club at Tranquility du Jour.

7. create something
The act of making something will allow you to feel a sense of completion and pride for bringing something new into the world. Knit a scarf, make a banner, craft a meal, write blog posts, sew a dress, or paint a watercolor postcard.

8. massage
Massage has many benefits and is the perfect antidote to achy muscles. If a spa isn't in the cards, consider a neck or foot rub at your neighborhood nail salon, check out the local massage school for good deals from therapists-in-training, or ask your beloved for a complimentary rub down.

8 Weekly Tools

1. plan week's MITs
These are your Most Important Tasks. Choose three to five tasks to focus on each week and align your daily actions with bringing these items to fruition. Let them be your week's roadmap.

2. soak in the tub
This grounding practice is incredibly therapeutic and helps to clear the mind after a long day. Light candles, play music, bring in a flute of bubbly or sparkling water, and allow yourself to melt into this sensual renewal practice.

3. take a digital day off
Grant yourself a sabbatical from being glued to technology. Spend time getting your hands dirty in the garden, baking a pie, reading a book, or collaging in your art journal. Our connection to technology needs the off switch from time to time.

4. clear clutter
Piles of paperwork become mountains when not handled regularly. Take time each week to reduce the clutter around you and watch yourself breathe easier and feel lighter.

5. pen a love note
Reach out to a friend, family member, pen pal, or even yourself {a letter to your past or future self} with a thoughtful note letting them know you're thinking of them and sending good thoughts. Include a bag of tea, article of interest, or token of love. This sweet gesture goes a long way in our fast-paced society.

6. buy or pick fresh flowers
Surround yourself with living color through potted plants, cut flowers, herbs, and bamboo stalks. If you have a garden, pick flowers and bring them into your living space to spruce up a barren bedside table.

7. take an artist date
Head out to a solo excursion to nurture your inner artist for one hour each week. Try a trip to a flower market, café, museum, bookstore, or art gallery, and watch your ideas flow.

8. savor a green juice
Infuse your body with healing nutrients found in a green juice. Watch your energy and vitality soar as get a "direct shot of vitamins, minerals, enzymes, protein, and oxygen," according to Kris Carr, author of *Crazy Sexy Diet*.

8 Daily Tools

1. morning routine
Greet your day with a sun salutation, cuppa tea, or brisk walk with your beloved four-legged friend. Begin each morning with an intentional, tranquil tone.

2. daily dress up
Let your daily dress reflect your personality, lifestyle, and signature style. Always add a dose of flair and don't forget your smile, good attitude, and vintage accessory.

3. mindful movement
Take a moment each day to move your body through dance, walking, sun salutations, or any other activity that makes your skin glisten. Bookend the experience with a dose of meditation by sitting still and connecting to your breath. Inhale, exhale, ommmm.

4. eat your veggies
Reduce animal product intake and increase plant-based consumption to have a joyful effect on your health, the planet, and animals.

5. journal
Spend a few moments penning morning pages, noting highlights from your day, recurring dreams, experiences, how you're feeling, or anything else on your mind. Use the journal prompts on your weekly layouts for inspiration.

6. goal review
Each day pull out and read over the dreams you penned for the month. This will help to ensure daily decisions are in alignment with the direction of your dreams.

7. gratitude
At the end of each day, find at least one thing for which you are grateful. It may be as simple as a warm bed, furry friend, or fresh water. Studies conducted over the past decade show that adults who frequently feel grateful have more energy, more optimism, more social connections, and more happiness than those who do not.

8. evening routine
End your day with reflection—write in your journal, shut down your computer and smart phone, soak in the tub, or read in bed for 30 minutes before lights out.

~ TRANQUILITY TOOLS TAKEAWAYS ~

~ CURRENT DAY IN THE LIFE ~

When reviewing my not-so-spacious Day in the Life schedule of February 2006 {on p. 106}, I noticed heaviness and palpitations in my chest. That period was fraught with overwork and an inability to bask in the tranquility I so desperately sought. Over the years I've learned that down time is a necessity, not a luxury.

Stepping away from the computer to curl up on a settee with a book and green juice one recent Saturday night, I acknowledged how far I'd come. In the past I'd work into the wee hours, trying to check one more thing off my to-do list. Now, I recognize my tired eyes, my not-so-clear thinking, and know that to-do will be waiting for me in the morning. So, I'll take a hot bath, curl up with a book, or go to bed at 9:30 p.m. Sure, age has something to do with this, but I'm hopeful that wisdom does, too. Here's a peek at my current schedule:

Monday

7:00 a.m. Rise and morning routine

8:30 a.m.—3:00 p.m. Writing, appointments, and online work

4:00 p.m.—10:00 p.m. Meetings, yoga, and teaching at Tranquil Space Dupont

10:00 p.m.—10:30 p.m. Evening routine

Tuesday

7:00 a.m. Rise and morning routine

8:30 a.m. Writing and online work

10:00 a.m. Appointment

Noon and 4:00 p.m. Teach at Tranquil Space Arlington, write in between

5:30 p.m. Home to regroup, handle emails, love on pets

7:30 p.m. Yoga at Tranquil Space Dupont

9:00 p.m.—10:00 p.m. Evening routine

Wednesday

7:00 a.m. Rise and morning routine

8:00 a.m. Writing and online work

9:00 a.m.—5:00 p.m. Meet with clients at the Women's Center

6:00 p.m.—10:00 p.m. Writing group, meditation class, or tea dates

10:00 p.m.—10:30 p.m. Evening routine

Thursday

7:00 a.m. Rise and morning routine

8:00 a.m. Writing and online work

9:00 a.m.—5:00 p.m. Meet with clients at the Women's Center

6:00 p.m.—10:00 p.m. Yoga and teaching at Tranquil Space Dupont

10:00 p.m.—10:30 p.m. Evening routine

Friday

7:00 a.m. Rise and morning routine

8:30 a.m.—4:00 p.m. Writing, appointments, studio meetings, and online work

4:00 p.m.—9:00 p.m. Yoga and teaching occasional workshops at Tranquil Space Dupont

9:00 p.m.—10:00 p.m. Evening routine

Saturday/Sunday

7:00 a.m. Rise and morning routine

8:30 a.m.—9:00 p.m. Writing, appointments, studio meetings, gym, brunch dates, reading, Artist Dates, theatre, yoga or meditation classes, online work, plan next week's MITs

9:00 p.m.—10:00 p.m. Evening routine

Morning routine may include:

Feed Le Pug and kitties, light candles, make and sip tea, review *Daybook*, soak in the tub, pen thoughts in journal, walk Le Pug, meditation, yoga, spritz self with *parfum*, scrape tongue, wash and moisturize face, brush teeth

Evening routine may include:

Curl up with a book, soak in the tub, light candles, make and sip tea, review *Daybook*, meditation, yoga, walk Le Pug, pen thoughts in journal, spritz self with *parfum,* scrape tongue, wash and moisturize face with face oil, brush teeth

~ 52 TRANQUILITY TIPS ~

Tranquility Tips are designed to pepper into your daily experience.

1. Nourish your body with slices of apple and almond butter.
2. List five things you're grateful for.
3. Sip water with a mint sprig.
4. Read The Artist's Way and ignite your creative spark.
5. Make a tea date with a longtime girlfriend.
6. Sprinkle bud vases with tiny flowers around your home.
7. Soak in a bubble-filled tub.
8. Take your journal and favorite pen to a local café to write.
9. Review your Year's Dreams and take one action step.
10. Snap a photo of something that brings you joy.
11. Light a candle and set your day's intention.
12. Wrap your hands around a hot cuppa tea and breathe deeply.
13. Collage your ideal day.
14. Create a comfort case: earplugs, eyemask, lavender spray, lip balm.
15. Dab lavender oil on your wrists.
16. Roll out your yoga mat and move through sun salutations.
17. Pen a love note to someone special.
18. Create something: knit armwarmers, make a meal, pen an essay.
19. Browse your bookshelf and reread a favorite.
20. Give a sampling of your resources—time, money, or energy—to a cause.
21. Host a tea party complete with macarons and cucumber mint sandwiches.
22. Nurture your nails with a jaunt to the salon for a mani pedi.

23. Go on an Artist Date: café, museum, art gallery, bookstore.
24. Savor a green juice filled with apple, spinach, cucumber, kale, and ginger.
25. Get out in nature for a jolt of fresh air.
26. Feel sunshine on your skin for a dose of Vitamin D.
27. Take a break from technology to create time and space.
28. Go through those tucked away drawers and get rid of clutter.
29. Add a fun accessory to your outfit: brooch, dangly earrings, scarf, smile.
30. Plan an upcoming jaunt away to experience something new to you.
31. Jot down your nighttime dreams and watch for patterns.
32. Close your eyes and take 10 deep breaths.
33. Rearrange your home or office for a shift in perspective.
34. Tote a bag of raw almonds with you for protein on-the-go.
35. Read the work of Pema Chödrön for thoughtful inspiration.
36. Review your Month's Dreams and take one action step.
37. Bake a batch of spicy kale chips {recipe on p. 200}.
38. Display objects that hold meaning for you.
39. Roll out your yoga mat mid-day and take a 20-minute savasana.
40. Write five thank you notes and insert a tea bag secured with Washi tape.
41. Go for a bike ride and feel the wind in your hair.
42. Pack a picnic and head to your nearest park with a book, journal, and pen.
43. Eat a meal slowly in silence and tune into the experience.
44. During downtime, tune your body versus reaching for your smartphone.
45. Try cutting products with added sugar out of your diet.
46. Make face oil with argan oil {2/3}, rosehip seed oil {1/3}, and rose essential oil {4-7 drops}.
47. Remember that the only way out of pain or challenge is through it.
48. Practice loving kindness toward yourself and those around you.
49. Accept what you cannot change.
50. Try eating 80% alkaline foods {ripe fruits, greens, sprouts, veggies}.
51. Listen intently to the person in front of you.
52. Make dreaming a regular part of your daily routine and make them big.

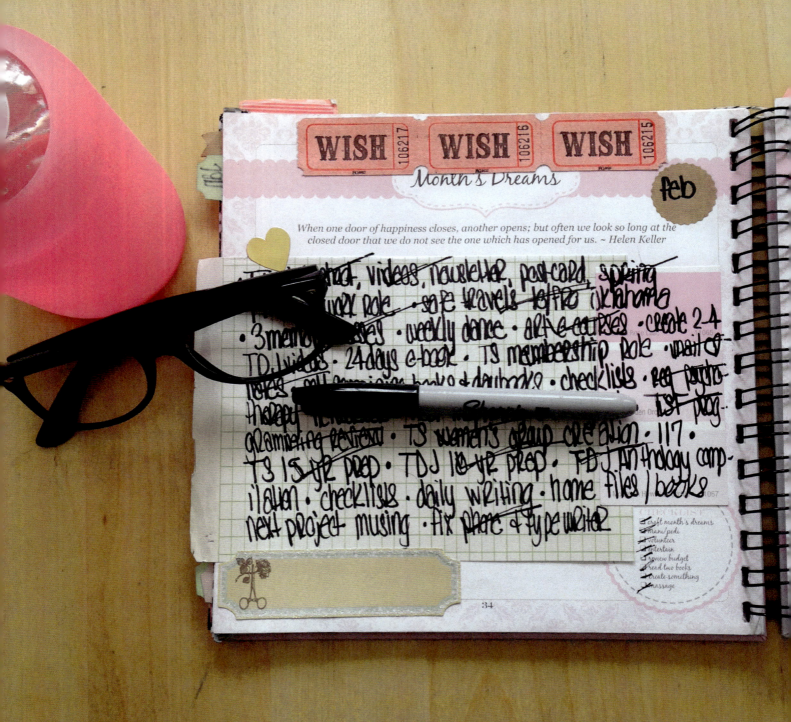

~ PEN MONTH'S DREAMS ~

At the start of each month, I have a ritual around reviewing and crafting my dreams. Below is a simple four-part process.

1. Review last month's dreams. Check off all you completed and acknowledge your efforts. Review what's left and decide whether you want to bring them over to the new month.

2. Gather creative tools to enhance your month's dreams. I tend to use an inspiring image pulled from a magazine along with a glue stick, washi tape, Sharpie, stamps, and stickers.

3. Layout your page. My background is simple with an image of stacked washi tapes, real washi tape, and a Kraft sticker. Feel free to collage with a few images, paint chips, doilies, maps, or vintage paper.

4. Add your dreams. Add any dreams from the previous month that weren't completed and still resonate. Add new ones for this month and consider not only to-dos, but to-bes. Pen what you want to read, write, cook, bake, wear, shed, express, forgive, try, clean, finish and, ultimately, experience.

Snap a pic and share your dreams on our Facebook page. It's inspiring to see one another's dreams in visual format. Happy dreaming.

~ GRATITUDE LIST ~

Pink legal pads
Striped socks
Lavender incense
Kale-infused juice
Spinach salad with walnuts + dried cranberries
Sunshine on my skin
Baby birds
Pigs in mud
Peonies
Pug snorts
Vanilla cupcakes
Rose macarons
Warm embrace
Pink bike
Twinkle lights
Fresh-baked cookies
Insightful documentaries
Writing classes
Free speech
Black leggings
Tutus
A well-loved journal
Colored ballpoint pens
String quartets
Houseboats
Kitten's purr
Polka-dot tights
Open windows
Crisp air
Crackling fire

Warm rain
Bubble baths
Snail mail
Hot cocoa w/marshmallows
Handmade bunting
Soft linens
Parents' love
India temple incense
Kind gestures
Smiling strangers
Steaming cuppa tea
Confetti
Yoga
Legs up the wall
Hip openers
Appreciation

Water with mint sprig
Stacks of books
Wood floors
Light-filled space
Stretchy clothing
Lip balm
Flowery perfume
Top knots
French café music
Fluffy pillows & blankets
Bed days
Cork yoga blocks
Theatre tickets
Vegan boots
Sunday mornings in bed
Hearing "I love you"

Create your own list.

~ TRANQUILITY THOUGHTS ~

For a Mindful Check-In

I am feeling _____. What I'm noticing in my body is _____.

My mind is focused on _____.

I'd like to be feeling more _____, and will take a small step toward that feeling by _____ _____ and _____.

For Seasonal Reflection

My intention for this season is _____.

By _____ {date}, I want to finish _____ _____, read _____ _____, clean _____, forgive _____, try _____ _____, make _____, write _____, cook/bake _____, feel _____

_____, wear _____,

express _____, let go of_____

_____, do _____

_____, be _____,

travel to_____, and experience

_____.

For Takeaway Capturing

I recently attended/completed/read _____

and I am _____ I did. My biggest takeaways were

_____, _____,

and _____. I plan to take these action

steps based on what I learned: _____,

_____, _____,

and _____. Because of this experience,

I will live my life differently by _____

_____.

~ KALE CHIPS ~

Oui, I've been doing damage in the kitchen for the first time in years.

Confession 1: I'm addicted to kale chips.

Confession 2: They are SUPER easy.

Here's my oh-so-easy how-to:

1. Pick up a big bag of kale and preheat oven to 350 degrees.

2. Remove heavy stalks to leave only leaves. Throw 1/3 of the big bag into a pan so the bottom is covered.

3. Toss kale in a few capfuls of oil.

4. Add heaps of yummy seasoning {try Montreal steak seasoning or nutritional yeast}.

5. Put on baking sheet. Bake 15 minutes.

6. Voilà, heaven awaits.

My mouth is watering simply typing up this how-to. Even Le Pug loves them. Happy kale chip consuming.

~ GREEN JUICE ~

This juice is high in fiber, low-calorie, and rich in vitamins.

Ingredients:

2 cups spinach   1 bunch parsley
2 cups cucumber   2 apples
1 head of celery   Juice of 1 lime
1/2 inch or tsp ginger root   Juice of 1/2 lemon

Directions:

Combine all ingredients in a blender. This makes approximately 28-30 ounces, or 3-4 servings.

Source: doctoroz.com

~ MORE READER FEEDBACK ~

Being a parent is never easy. Being a single mom to two girls is double the fun and double the trouble. So when my daughters hit the teens, my stress level went up. Add to that working in the airline industry. Not a great combination for a serene lifestyle. I happened to come across Kimberly's podcast one day. One listen and I was hooked. Her soothing voice discussing simple ways to make my life a little less hectic and more beautiful was like standing under a waterfall on a hot, summer day. Daily doses of her blog showed me that while my life 'outside' could be filled with craziness, I could make my 'inside' life a lot nicer.

From Kimberly, I have learned it's not always the grand gestures which make a difference in my life, but the little things. Simple things, like a lovely flower in a Mason jar, can take a day from dull and dismal to bright and sweet. She reminds me to breathe and to be creative in my everyday life. I am reminded of these lessons every day when I open my *Tranquility du Jour Daybook*.

I have watched Kimberly grow from a simple blog and podcast, to a globetrotting tranquility guru, bringing loads of inspiration and comfort to thousands. My daughters are now 23 and 21, and I have passed on not only the podcasts and blog to them, but also her books. My hope is they will take her messages to heart and not have to go through many of the things I did in order to become even more wonderful women.

Judy Hudgins, Montana
knottyneedle.blogspot.com

We all go through those times in life. The tough times that zap your creativity and *joie de vivre*. For me, it was the year that I finished my Ph.D. under tough circumstances. I worked round the clock—lost my grandmother—nearly lost my sister—drove into the underbelly of semi-truck—hobbled on crutches—and became a shell of the spunky girl whom I used to be. It wasn't right away, but slowly, life beckoned me back.

I was sitting at my desk, staring at a stack of phone messages that I needed to return when I saw Kimberly's post from an art retreat in Mexico. I was entranced. That is where I wanted to be. That is the life I wanted to live. I was inspired.

Everyday a burst of happiness came over me as I saw her blog alert come into my mailbox. Mindfulness. Yoga. Healthy living. Creative expression. Creative organizing. Goal setting. Authentic living. Freedom to explore this beautiful world with the eyes of an artist. A woman who was unashamed of living the life of her dreams.

Tranquility du Jour resonated and awaked the spunky creative kid inside of me that had been crushed by the weight of professional adulthood. Life unfolded. I followed Kimberly's book suggestions {*The Artist's Way, Life is a Verb, 12 Secrets of Highly Creative Women*}. I took in new approaches to living a creative life. An inspired journey of wholeness bloomed. I connected with savvy soul sisters. Possibilities sprouted—amazing opportunities bloomed. I took up belly dance. I beame a yoga teacher. I journaled. I traveled. I created. I followed Kimberly's leads to *The Right-Brain Business Plan* and the Sketchbook Project. I joined a farm club. I collaged . . . everything in sight. I meditated. I helped others find their authentic voice. I lit candles and savored times of self-reflection. I volunteered with animals. I made monthly and seasonal goals. I learned to be good to myself. I let life sparkle.

I'm so grateful for the world, Kimberly unveiled within me and around me. In your hands you hold a treasure of inspiration. It is rare to find an authentic teacher—so gracious in sharing resources—self-less and motivated to help each of us create our own life of joy and fullness. My deepest hope is that this *Tranquility du Jour Anthology* opens up doors of inspiration for you as it has for me. Kimberly's life and work gives us each permission to shine, sparkle, dance, and live life with intention and deep gratitude. *Bisous!*

Dr. Bobbie Legg, Utah

I stumbled across Kimberly Wilson and *Tranquillity du Jour* in 2008. I didn't know it at that stage, but my life was about to be made significantly better.

At the time I was coming out from a rock bottom experience. Severe anxiety had drowned my light and after a massive decision about life, my soul was searching for sparkle, inspiration, and ways to grow. Enter *Tranquility du Jour* . . .

I devoured the content. I felt Kimberly spoke directly to me and what I needed to hear. The chandeliers, Francophile-themes, feline and canine companions—right up my alley. And the podcasts. Oh the podcasts. The episodes whispered into my ears, helping me to acknowledge the beauty of life and I have scribbled pages and pages of notes, aha's and learnings from the amazing guests over the years.

One of my favourite parts is the Week In Review post. They are a balm to occasional inertia and inspiration to get things done! I've included this habit into some of my posts and the ripple effect has been tremendous.

Through the community I have met some amazing women, spread out all across the world, that I have the honour to call friends now.

Morning Pages, yoga and self-care rituals all infuse my life now and that has a lot to do with the people in the Pink Palace and *Tranquility du Jour*.

Thank you for being one of the conduits that helped me to reconnect to who I am and what my passions are. Your posts are so much more than words on a page. I'm now on a path that helps others discover more of who they are and to show up and shine bright in their own worlds. Heartfelt gratitude for what you put out into the world and the positive impact it has.

Arienne Gorlach, Australia
ariennegorlach.com

~ PHOTO CREDITS ~

Photography taken by Kimberly's iPhone. p. 12, Hiking, Steve Wilson. p. 30, Tattoo, Tim Mooney. p. 32, Gramma, Linda Wilson. p. 124, Feeding Cows, Sally Boardman. p. 129, Chalkboard, Tim Mooney. p. 132, Cow, Tim Mooney. p. 135, Pig, Tim Money. p. 150, Smelling Roses, Denise Nieman. p. 213, Pig and Pug, Tim Mooney. p. 213, Ballerina, Linda Wilson.

~ INDEX ~

17th Street 126
accessories 24
Acknowledgments 210
action steps 159
activism 9, 11, 69, 121, 123, 128, 133, 137
activists 36, 91
acupuncture 11
ahimsa 103
Air Supply 22, 31
Alaska 169
alignment 106, 149
Allen, James 107
ambiance 131
Amtrak 19, 34
animals 24, 69, 96, 115, 128, 134, 145, 146
ankle rolls 52
anthology 10
aparigraha 123
apes 136
April 16, 58, 86, 143, 169
Arlington 17, 34, 111
Arizona 172
art 10, 70

Art and Asana Retreat 19
Art + Yoga Retreat 19
Art journal toolkit 19
art journal 85, 89, 152
art journaling 9, 18, 89, 146, 168
Artist Date 70, 91, 92, 96
Artist's Way, The 85, 95, 102
asana 74
Ashtanga 62
ASPCA 126
August 71, 80, 110, 126, 129, 150, 167
authenticity 55
backbends 48, 57
balance 112, 154
ballet 17
bamboo 142
Barre 50
bath 49, 106, 107
bathtub 159, 174
Becker, Holly 91
Belsky, Scott 77, 114
blog 10, 15, 34, 70, 72, 76, 85, 88, 92, 106, 107, 110, 128, 160, 170, 171
blogging 10, 17, 176
Bonnard 35, 37, 39, 40, 41, 169
Bourke-White, Margaret 80
Brach, Tara 87
brand 107
Bravo, Britt 94
Breathnach, Sarah 103
Brown, Brene 114
Brown, Jenny 36
boxing 29
Buddha 147
Buddhism 24
business plan 89
Butler, Amy 24
Butterfly, Julia 36
café 29, 62, 72, 97, 116, 151, 160, 161, 168, 172
Calgary 171
camper 40, 160, 161, 164, 165, 169, 174, 176
camping 23, 164
Canada 170

Canadian Rockies 176
candles 23, 49, 58, 67, 174, 175
Cameron, Julia 85, 95
Carver, Courtney 73
Castellane 160
Cezanne, Jackson 19
chair twists 51
Chanel 22
chamomile tea 31
Champagne, Marie 131
chandelier 67, 111, 164
ChariTea 125
charities 103
chaturanga 55, 56, 143
checklists 94
Chelsea Tattoo Company 31
child's pose 59
chimps 136
chocolate 22
Chödrön, Pema 139, 143, 183
Christmas 75
Christmas Eve 35
clutter 23, 24

collage 87, 90, 95, 159

Colorado 16

communicate 70

communication 61, 62, 127, 131

community 63, 113, 123, 124, 133

compassion 55, 118, 127, 131

compassionate 134, 143

conference 53, 88, 112, 122

confidence 63

Conway, Susannah 114, 115

Cope, Stephen 74

Cornwell, Melissa 158

Costa Rica 17, 20, 128, 162

Couch, Lillian Myrtle Stotlar Ewing 32

Creative and Conscious Business e-course 92

Creative Circle 89

creativity 11, 85, 90, 97, 103, 133

daily dress up 73

Dalai Lama 130

Daniels, Kristi 90

Darca 145

Das, Krishna 60

Day, Alison 105

Daybook 36, 78, 79, 95, 152, 166, 171

December 37, 57, 73, 78, 94, 95, 102, 108, 143, 145, 175

Deia 158

DIY 9

dosha 22

downtime 76, 77

downward-facing dog 47, 56

dristi 56

Dupont Circle 15, 17, 102, 110, 126

eagle arms 52

e-course 19, 78, 109

edge 54

emergenC 68

Emerson, Ralph Waldo 55

empowerment 55

E-Myth 112

Engelbreit, Mary 16

entrepreneur 101

entrepreneurship 11, 101, 118

essential oil 58

Etsy 23, 90, 110

exercise 96

eye pillow 31, 58, 69

Facebook 33, 75, 92, 130, 160

Farm Sanctuary 19, 126, 134, 135, 136, 170, 171, 172, 173

fashion 10

February 31, 43, 74, 87, 106, 109, 153, 154

Feeny, Melanie 18

Fisher, Eileen 21

flanerie 76

Fossey, Dian 136

France 67, 72, 115, 160, 166

Frank, Anne 121

Franks, Lynne 159

French 17, 76, 161

Friends of the Animals 125

Gandhi 129

Gannon, Sharon 24, 134, 136

Gates, Melinda 24

Gehlhar, Mary 116

George Washington University 17, 23, 89, 113

Georgetown University 16

gift bag 23

gifts 49

glamping 164, 165, 171

goals 36, 89

Gordhamer, Soren 149

gorillas 136

Gorloch, Arienne 203

Graham, Martha 97

Gramma 10, 19, 24, 31, 33, 34, 39, 41, 67, 75, 79

Grand Canyon 172, 174, 176

grateful 68, 72

gratitude 149, 168

Graves, Robert 158

green juice 81, 200

green smoothies 24

Greenpeace 126

grief 32, 40

Guillebeau, Chris 114

Hanh, Thich Nhat 52

handstand 57

Harrison, Scott 114

headstand 48, 49, 63

Hepburn, Audrey 24

hip-opening 57

Hip Tranquil Chick 9, 11, 17, 18, 69, 89, 105

hollydaze 35, 97, 172, 176

Hotel Chelsea 31

Howell, Kylie Grethen 79

Hudgins, Judy 200
Ibiza 43
Idaho 170, 171
ideas book 85, 88, 96
incense 67, 192
India 19, 24, 39, 163
inspiration 10, 88, 167
inspiration boards 23
Instagram 92, 152, 153, 160
Institute for Humane Education 129
Integrative Yoga Therapy 62
intention 49, 55, 81, 107, 123, 165, 188
internship 75, 132
inversions 55, 57
Iyer, Pico 157
Jackson 171
January 41, 50, 51, 59, 68, 81, 89, 125
Japanese masking tape 75, 89
Jewel 181
Jivamukti 35, 60, 97, 122, 136
Jobs, Steve 24
Johnson, Betsey 167
Joshua Tree National Park 173
journal 16, 23, 35, 49, 77, 80, 91, 144, 167, 185, 187, 188, 192
journaling 85, 93
July 21, 37, 56, 70, 104, 112, 114, 122, 147
June 72, 93, 104, 117, 150, 160
Kabat-Zinn, Jon 19, 141
kale chips 67, 95, 200

Kripalu 109, 145
Kumar, Sameet 33
Kundalini 158
LaPorte, Danielle 114
Lasater, Judith 80
lifestyle 11, 15, 67, 104
Le Beau 17, 19, 20, 23, 24, 31, 33, 35, 39, 41, 60, 62, 72, 106, 107, 111, 126, 128, 134, 152, 158, 159, 160, 161, 163, 164, 169, 171, 172, 173, 175, 176
Le Pug 17, 22, 23, 33, 35, 37, 39, 40, 68, 72, 87, 106, 126, 160, 161, 163, 167, 169, 171, 172, 173, 174, 175, 176
legacy 70
Legg, Bobbie 203
legs up the wall 57, 58, 144, 192

Lennon, John 148
Leonsis, Ted 22
lifestyle 54, 55, 69
lion's breath 31
lip balm 69
Lokah Samastah Sukhino Bhavantu 30, 62, 129, 136
love notes 76, 87, 90
LUSH 22
Madonna 24, 73
Mallorca 43, 157, 158
Mama Wilson 36, 40, 69, 75, 131, 164
March 33, 91, 113, 128, 132, 134
marketing 110, 114
marking 59
Matisse 169

May 20, 22, 29, 30, 53, 54, 60, 61, 75, 88, 115, 122, 128, 149, 164, 165, 166, 168
Meatless Mondays 69
Meatout 136
meditate 90
meditation 23, 77, 80, 81, 127, 142, 143, 149, 158, 159
Mexico 85, 109, 198
Mid-Atlantic Pug Rescue 125
Miller, Henry 181
Milwaukee 53
mindful 194
Mindful Monday 10, 69, 118
Mindful money management 55
mindful movement 77, 185
mindfulness 9, 10, 11, 19, 52, 78, 123, 141, 142, 144, 145, 146, 149, 153, 154
Miss Lillie 40, 169, 171, 172, 175, 176
MITs 79
moderation 55
Moffitt, Phillip 35, 149
monkey mind 157
Montreal 30
mood boards 92
Moon, Amanda Michelle 89
Moran, Victoria 19
Morning Pages 96, 171
morning routine 59
Muir Woods 24, 172
My Sister's Place 125
My Story 11
N Street Village 19
nag champa incense 23, 31

naps 77, 127
National Yoga Month 62
neck rolls 51
New Hampshire 90
New Mexico 173
New York 91
New York City 23, 167
Nin, Anais 15, 102, 103, 157, 179, 182
niyamas 74
no-intent 77
Noe, Alva 148
Not So Big Life, The 87, 144
not so big life 145
November 76, 116, 158, 163, 172, 174, 175
Nuggets 12, 44, 63, 83, 98, 118, 137, 154, 176
NYC 30, 35, 91, 95, 171
obituary 32
October 91, 104, 134, 142, 170, 172
office yoga 48, 51
Oklahoma 16, 30, 33, 73, 116, 153, 172, 173
Oklahoma, University of 16
Olive Garden 22, 174
online courses 92
orangutan 135, 136, 137
Osho 85
Outer Banks 173, 175
P Street 17, 23, 108
Pacific Coast Highway 176
paint 49
Papaya art journal 93
parasailing 43, 44
Paris 18, 19, 23, 76, 79, 80, 150, 157, 166, 168

Paris + Provence 129
passion 55
Patanjali 123
Penna, Maite 124
Pennebaker, James 89
perfectionism 152
pet loss 40
Pickard, Catherine 133
pigs 22, 136, 137, 174
Pigs Animal Sanctuary 19, 130
Pink Palace 17, 67, 78, 112, 172, 173
Planner Pad 23
podcasts 16, 19, 21, 34, 67, 73, 85, 89, 90, 101, 109, 121, 133, 141, 157, 170
Pollan, Michael 123
Pop-Ups 9, 92, 169, 172
pratyahara 80, 117
Project 333 73
Provence 160, 169
Rainbow Bridge 40
recycle 123
Red Apes 126
Redwoods 173, 174
reflect 70
reflection 10, 49, 74, 115, 123, 146
relationships 41, 44, 53, 113, 150, 152
resolutions 81
restorative sequence 58
retreat 90, 109, 165
Roach, Geshe Michael 60
Roffer, Robin Fisher 150
Roosevelt, Eleanor 67
Rumi 146

Sager, Gina 142
Salon de Provence 161
Salzberg, Sharon 81
samskaras 36
Sanskrit 30
SARK 21
savasana 48, 53, 54, 57, 110
Savvy Sources 11
saucha 74
schedule 71, 109, 110
Schultz, Howard 113
seated cat/cow 51
seated child's pose 52
self-awareness 77
self-care 34, 35, 36, 37, 55, 148
self-nurturing 55
September 62, 69, 130, 169
Shapiro, Danny 81
Sheehy, Gail 34
shoulder rolls 51
signature style 15, 73
Silverthrone Recreation Center 47
simplicity 78
small shifts 87
snail mail 75, 76
soccer 22
spacious 71
spaciousness 67, 96
Spain 17, 43, 157
spiritual activism 122
spiritual activist 121
spirituality 70, 96, 123
Squam 90
Squam Art Retreat 90

Starbucks 29, 113, 126, 171
Starr, Mary Catherine 19, 95, 117
stationery 76
Stewart, Martha 21, 24, 182
Stringer, Dave 53, 54
Strom, Max 61
style 70, 72
Sullivan, Rosemary 182
sun salutations 57
surgery 29
Susanka, Sarah 145
synchronicity 35
Tacinelli, Darlynn 58
tadasana 49, 57
Target 73
Taos 173
tattoo 30
Tazo 22, 29
teacher training 17, 54, 109, 122, 136
Tharp, Twyla 179
Throat Coat 68
tigers 139
tranquil 161
Tranquil Teens 21, 23, 125
Tranquil Space 11, 15, 17, 20, 22, 34, 37, 41, 43, 54, 55, 85, 86, 87, 91, 101, 102, 103, 108, 109, 110, 111, 113, 115, 117, 118, 125, 126, 128, 169, 172, 173, 176
Tranquil Space Foundation 17, 34, 94, 109, 115, 122, 125, 128, 170, 173, 176
Tranquilista 9, 18, 22, 87, 101, 125
TranquiliT 17, 18, 21, 24, 34, 69, 70, 73, 86, 87, 101, 103, 104, 109, 112, 115, 116, 144, 165, 176

TranquiliT manifesto 53
TranquiliT Thoughts 9, 15
TranquiliT.com 116
tranquility 10, 11, 12, 52, 58, 67, 70, 75, 80, 128, 133, 141, 169
Tranquility du Jour 8, 10, 11, 12, 67, 69, 72, 73, 79, 89, 90, 92, 104, 115, 124, 129, 133, 145, 150, 167, 171
Tranquility du Jour Daybook 19, 35, 73, 85, 92, 94, 165
Tranquility Timeline 16
Tranquility Tip 69, 188
Tranquility Tools 183
Tranquility Tour 9, 11, 19, 40, 42, 76, 78, 134, 157, 164, 170, 172, 173, 174, 175
Tranquilologie 9, 19, 36, 77, 80, 92, 94, 176
Tranquilosophy 35, 128
transform 63
transition 35
travel 11, 42, 96, 110, 116, 133, 146, 165, 176
tree pose 49

Trees for the Future 125
triangle 54
turtles 24, 125, 135, 136, 137
Twitter 92, 152
unplugging 67, 76, 77
upward-facing dog 56
utkatasana 54
vacation 80
vata 142
vegan 149, 167
Vegan Academy 19, 36
vegetarian 123
Verdon, Gorges du 160
Victore, James 153
Virginia 172
vision board 90

visual journaling 23, 88
volunteer 123, 130, 131
volunteering 123
Walker, Alice 122
walking meditation 52
Warson, Elizabeth 89
Washington, D.C. 43, 86, 102, 121
Washington Humane Society 125, 132
Waterton National Park 171
Wednesday Well-Being 69
Week in Review 10, 34, 58
weekend wish list 58
Weil, Zoe 129
Wild Woman Workshop 16
Wisconsin 54

Women's Business Center 117
Woodstock Animal Sanctuary 36
World Domination Summit 19, 94, 114
wrist rolls 52
writing 97, 103
Wulfert, Kimberly 170
Wyoming 171, 174
yamas 74
Yee, Rodney 53
yin yoga 90
yoga 9, 10, 11, 15, 16, 20, 23, 29, 36, 42, 47, 48, 49, 51, 53, 54, 55, 57, 59, 62, 79, 81, 86, 96, 102, 103, 104, 106, 109, 110, 116, 117, 122, 124, 133, 134, 142, 144, 149, 158, 159, 167, 168
Yoga at Kimberly's 117
yoga studio 11, 73, 108, 109, 145
Yoga Sutras 60, 123
yoga teacher training 16
Zen Princess 23

Acknowledgements

Many special beings helped make this *Anthology* possible, including:

Le Beau, Tim Mooney, who is my best friend, cheerleader, and right hand.

Mama, Linda Wilson, who regularly and gleefully proclaims that I'm her favorite daughter in the whole wide world. {Author's note: I'm her *only* daughter}.

Pops, Steve Wilson, who inspired the writing craft and love of photography at an early age.

Le Pug, Louis Wilson Mooney, who constantly brings a smile to my face.

Teams at Tranquil Space, TranquiliT, and Tranquil Space Foundation, who keep me inspired with their passion for spreading tranquility.

Beloved Carol Meyers who reviewed and inspired this collection of posts.

Designer Christy Jenkins for her impressive way of bringing my vision to life complete with pink, damask, and chandeliers.

Editors Jen Safrey, Gina Carpellotti, and Darca for helping crystallize my sometimes oh-so-rambling message.

Beta readers Catherine Emily Pickard, Nicole Carlson, Darlynn Tacinelli, Charissa Struble, Kate Gunn Pagel, Shira Engel, Alison Day, Hope Bordeaux, Amanda Moon, Kristi Daniels, Melissa Cornwell.

Blog readers, podcast listeners, retreaters, e-course participants, TranquiliT shoppers, and yoga students, your support has made this decade possible. I bow to you.

Le Pug

Mama + Pops

Le Beau

About the Author

Kimberly Wilson is a lover of Paris, snail mail, and nude-colored manis with a penchant for piles of books and rose macarons. She founded Tranquil Space—named among the top 25 yoga studios in the world by *Travel + Leisure*, penned *Hip Tranquil Chick*, *Tranquilista*, and *Tranquilologie*, and designs a locally-sewn eco-fashion line, TranquiliT.

Kimberly holds master's degrees in women's studies and social work, co-launched Tranquil Space Foundation, and is a pre-licensed therapist at The Women's Center. She is also a cheerleader for animal rights and passionate about pigs.

You'll often find her sipping fragrant tea, practicing yoga on a leopard-print mat, or leading retreats around the world. Her work has been featured in numerous books, *Daily Candy*, *Washingtonian*, *Yoga Journal*, and *Fast Company*.

She lives in a petite Pink Palace in Washington, D.C. with two rescue kitties, Le Beau, and Le Pug. Indulge in "tranquilosophy" via Kimberly's blog and podcast, *Tranquility du Jour*, and online courses.

Made in the USA
Las Vegas, NV
11 October 2022